by

Larry Yeagley

520 N. Stine Rd.

Charlotte, MI 48813

TABLE OF CONTENTS

Prologue

Thousands of volumes in Yale Divinity School's library lured me to the dark stacks. If only I had enough books at my fingertips, I could produce life-enriching sermons. Weeks with the books soon proved my youthful dream to be an illusion. The hurting people in my parish called me to their places of pain. There I found my laboratory of practical theology.

As my ministry to grieving people intensified, I went to the consultants and scholars, but only a fraction of their advice remained in my mental memory bank. Theories are seldom retained.

Men, women and children engulfed in the paralyzing emptiness of grief were my living textbooks. As I entered their pain, they opened their lives to me. We hurt together. We learned together. We found restoration together. This was the laboratory of brokenness.

We spent little time on theory. The raw realities of disconnectedness spoke to us. The non-essentials and the superficialities of the social and religious worlds were discarded. Pain and loneliness drove us to the heart of life's priorities. Focusing on those priorities brought the resurrection of hope.

I walked through human loss with people of many backgrounds. Their stories are written indelibly upon my mind. My character has been intricately fashioned by their tragedy and transformation. Erasing their imprints on my life is impossible. They are vivid in my dreams and daily reflections, not in a morbid sense, but in relation to my thoughts of human triumph.

Graduates from the school of human brokenness speak to you in this volume. Behind the author's name are hundreds of authorities on grief who must remain anonymous. Their anonymity does not diminish the force of their message.

1

Grief Hurts

Martha was hospitalized for eight days with acute abdominal pain. Her physician concluded that there must be a stressful situation causing the pain. I was asked to visit Martha.

She couldn't put her finger on any major changes in her life over the last year. By careful questioning I encouraged her to reflect on her past experiences. As she moved back year by year, her body language portrayed more and more stress. Finally she told me about her eleven-year-old daughter who died eight years earlier. She was upset about her death, but she swallowed and choked back the tears.

"It must have been a very sad time in your home when Kim died," I commented.

"Yes, it was, Chaplain, but I never cried, not even at the funeral."

"I don't understand how you could refrain from crying," I answered.

"It wasn't easy at first. You see, my family scolded me every time I began to cry. If they saw my chin quiver they'd tell me to stop it." She was noticeably ready to cry as she spoke to me.

I was very interested in the details of Kim's death, so I encouraged Martha to tell me how it happened.

The story poured out freely. I had the feeling that she hadn't discussed it with anyone for years.

"Martha," I said quietly, "I am not your family. I am giving you permmission to weep. Please don't hold the tears any longer. It won't make me uncomfortable to see you cry."

At this invitation, Martha began to weep for the first time in eight years. The dam finally burst and let the pain of all those years come flowing out.

We spent an hour together. Then she wiped her eyes one more time and said with a sigh, "Oh, I feel so relieved. You'll never know what a heavy load this has been to carry all this time. I really thank you for listening and putting up with my bawling."

"Martha, it has been a rewarding experience for me," I responded. "Now, please promise me that when you get home from the hospital you'll go up to your attic and open that old trunk. I want you to pull out all those baby clothes, toys, and paper dolls. Kiss them as you think about all the good times you and Kim had playing together. And if you can't cry, pray for God to give you tears."

"How did you know I had a trunk in the attic?" she asked with a surprised look on her face.

"I didn't, it was just a hunch," I assured her.

The trunk in the attic was a hunch, but the cause of her pain wasn't. I suspected all along that beneath her acute pain was unresolved grief.

The pain of grief is due to a major assault on the entire system. Our life script does not call for a child to die in her sleep. It does not include an unexpected announcement of divorce intentions. The script does not have a cancer diagnosis in it. We don't program highway fatalities into our life story. When life and the script suddenly collide there is onset of acute pain that cannot be prevented.

My parents lost six children, but I didn't appreciate their pain until my son was killed suddenly in a highway accident. I had been conducting bereavement support groups for four years when the tragedy struck, but the pain was a totally new experience for me. I was not prepared for that pain. There wasn't another human being who could bear that pain for me. It was my pain. It was unique. At times it frightened me.

My pain colored everything I did for many months. I remember sitting in a psychiatric care committee when the phone rang. A friend answered the phone and said it was for me. My face turned pale. The chief of psychiatry came to the phone to make sure I was alright. He relaxed when I told him it was not another emergency. I felt sudden pain when I knew the call was for me. It took a long time for the pain to subside.

Emotional pain is so powerful during acute grief that fear, anger and tears can manifest themselves instantly. People have told me about crying as they pushed the cart through the grocery store and becoming angry at people for minor annoyances. A very dear friend of mine trembled deep inside for many weeks after her child died.

Grief hurts us physically. While we can't link specific disorders and bereavement through controlled studies, it is widely accepted that bereavement may exacerbate existing illnesses and precipitate behaviors that leave people open to infectious diseases. This was the concluding opinion of the editors of a report published by National Academy Press. (Bereavement-Reactions, Consequences, and Care, Marion Osterweis, Fredric Solomon, and Morris Green, Editors. National Academy Press, Washington, D. C. 1984)

I am not into research, but many of the people who attended support groups with me have reported increased illnesses of a minor nature and the worsening of preexisting conditions.

The words bereave and rob are derived from the same root. When we lose an important relationship it feels like robbery, like someone has been ripped away from us.

Back in the 1950's I had surgery. The incision was covered with a bandage secured to my abdomen with strips of adhesive tape. Those were the days when you stayed in the hospital until you were well enough to go home and the tape stayed on until the hair began to grow out. The doctor assured me that ripping the tape off quickly was less painful than doing it bit by bit. I still question his theory, but I will never question the idea that having a loved one ripped away causes instant, excruciating pain.

Grief brings pain to families. The whole family system is out of balance. Confusion over roles and trying to fill the empty space left by the loss are just two of the sources of pain.

For months after a loss you sit across the table from family members who hurt just as you do. You find yourself confused with feelings of wanting someone to help you and wanting to help the people sitting across from you.

I distinctly remember walking out in the back yard a couple of weeks after my son died. My youngest son was raking the leaves. I saw the pain on his face and wanted to take it all away, but at the same time I wanted someone to take my pain away. As I looked at my wife and my sons my pain increased. I wanted to heal them, but I was powerless.

The first Christmas after the death was a disaster in our family. My wife and I went to the store to do some last minute shopping while the three boys put up the tree. When we came home the tree was all decorated, but the boys were in their rooms instead of lying on the floor looking at the lights as they usually did.

Jeff traditionally put the lights on the tree, but he wasn't there to do it. Filling that role was painful for the boys. Disagreements arose, but the trimmings were installed as best they could. At one point one of the boys tripped over the cord and the tree toppled, making it necessary to rearrange many of the ornaments. I still fight tears when I think of that painful evening.

I spent fourteen years as a chaplain in medical centers. I worked with patients in alcohol and drug rehabilitation programs, in medical-surgical units, in eating disorders programs, in psychiatric wards, in critical care units and in oncology units. During that time I noticed that unresolved grief inhibited the healing process.

Erich Lindemann's study of the victims of the Coconut Grove fire in Boston revealed the same conclusion. Those who were burned and lost a loved one in the fire healed measurably slower than those who were burned but had not lost a loved one.

One day I visited a woman who had just had brain surgery. When she learned that I was a chaplain she asked me to pray for her because she had just buried her daughter eight weeks ago.

"She died of cancer. She was so young. Oh, I lost my girl," the woman cried. She wept openly as I held her hand and spoke to her in an assuring voice.

I was concerned about how crying would affect her so soon after surgery, but I also noticed that as she wept she became more relaxed. There was a definite release of tension.

A young physician entered the room and told her not to cry, but when I told him that her girl died of cancer eight weeks ago, he left the room. Later he apologized for intruding. He said he was not aware of her recent loss. He felt that grieving freely was appropriate.

I have since been with dozens of post-surgery patients and permitted them to weep. Usually they express gratitude in a fashion similar to the woman who had brain surgery- "Thank you so much for talking to me. It helps."

In my reading I have discovered that the head nurse, the young physician and I were on the right track. The resolution of grief enhances the healing process.

I've heard it said that acute grief is like the common cold, ignore it and it will go away. I don't believe that's true. We now know that the common cold can lead to serious complications if proper care is not given. While grief is common to all people and is the normal process of bringing life back into focus after a great loss, it can lead to serious disorders without proper supportive care.

Helpful Exercises

1. Write a chronological list of losses you have experienced.

2. On a separate sheet of paper describe the pain you experienced during your most recent loss.

3. Select what you consider to be the most serious loss. Document how the pain of that loss affected your family and your personal health.

4. Mark the losses to which you are still adjusting. List them according to the amount of pain they are causing you now.

2

Why Is It So Hard?

When I lived in Battle Creek, Michigan, I observed a constant demonstration of one of the factors that makes grieving difficult. Large industries and a huge government installation were expert at the practice of transferring employees.

Some of the families that transferred into the area had been moved a half dozen times or more. Every move pulled up their roots. Eventually they defended themselves from the hurt by refusing to put down deep roots. As a result, their circle of supporting and intimate relationships was so narrowed that they had few people to lean on in times of crisis.

Recovery from the loss of a loved one hinges on the development and renewing of relationships that satisfy the basic human hungers. When fear of being hurt again prevents a family from forming an adequate support system, grief can be a nightmarish experience.

Churches traditionally have been the providers of supporting relationships, but this is no longer true in many cases. The parish, once a group of people living in the same area of a city and worshipping in the same church, has become a thing of the past. The sprawling suburbs have absorbed the people. Members of a congregation now are scattered and travel considerable distances to get to church. Contacts outside of weekend services are rare. Strong individualism taught by many religions has eroded the sense of community. Many people come to church for what they can get for themselves. The principle of servanthood has weakened. This further reduces the circle of supporting relationships.

Funeral services have been removed from the church and all of the religious symbolism and ritual pertaining to the church. Now we conduct funerals in what some believe to be a very sterile environment. Years ago the family celebrated infant dedication, baptism, marriage and death in the setting of worship. Today we plead convenience, economic savings, and making it easier for the family to worhip again as reasons for going to the funeral parlor.

I commend a friend of mine for establishing an alternative funeral business. He arranges funerals in churches, lodge halls, living rooms and gardens. Any place that has important memories and symbolism for the family. I conducted a funeral in which the person who had died was placed on a day bed, dressed in his favorite pajamas and robe.

Our society has removed death from the home. Dying people are placed in intensive care units where they die with machines and technicians around them. Their families are relegated to a little waiting room where their anxiety levels often skyrocket. After death occurs and the body is prepared, they are invited to view the dead.

I still remember a patient who was hooked up to a life-support system. The family tired of the long ordeal and went home to rest. When they finally made the decision to discontinue the heroics, they were too emotionally drained to go to his room. I sat by that man's bed, held his hand and watched the monitor until there was nothing but a straight line.

This practice makes family members feel helpless and useless. Some of them attend therapy groups after the funeral and cry, "If only I had been able to do more." Their grief is inhibited by guilt produced largely by separation from dying loved ones.

A woman complained to a therapist that she felt cut off from her husband. Her husband was slowly dying in a long-term care facility. The nursing staff discouraged her from any contact with her husband. She desperately wanted to rub soothing lotion on his dry arms, but permission was denied. She felt that her husband was rapidly becoming a total stranger to her. Imagine the difficulty in grieving that awaited her after her husband's death.

Hopefully the hospice movement will continue to maintain a fresh humanitarianism now that it is more integrated into the health care delivery system. One of the most important components of hospice is teaching family members to care for a dying relative in conjunction with adequate professional assistance. This will definitely facilitate the grieving process.

The increased number of persons dying at home under hospice care should reduce the fear of death and make it easier for people to be with the dying.

I had just finished my classes with a group of hospice consultants in Orlando and was riding back to the airport in a limousine. The driver looked over at me and said, "I don't know an awful lot about hospice, but I do know that I've never been afraid o' dyin'."

"Why is that?" I inquired.

"Well you see," he drawled, "I was reared in Appalachia where we do what we call 'sittin' up with.' A feller never dies alone where I come from - never."

"Could you tell me what 'sittin' up with' is all about?" I asked.

"Well, when a feller's a dyin', all the family, friends and neighbors take turns sittin' at the bedside until he dies. You're never afraid o' dyin' 'cause you know you'll never die alone. And after a feller's gone it's not near as hard to take 'cause you know you did all you could."

This is a lesson that many Americans have not learned yet.

When they do, the adjustment to loss will occur more easily.

Grief is hampered by the societal tendency to deny death. We have invented scores of euphemisms for the word death. It is treated like a four letter word. If you don't believe it, read the church bulletin or listen to the pastoral announcement of a death in the congregation. Drop in on a nursing conference and hear the words like passing and expired.

I worked in a hospital for ten weeks before I found out how the bodies were taken from the room to the morgue. The average visitor would never know that death happens in a hospital were it not for the newspaper obituaries.

Americans are masters at denial of death. This has not accommodated those who grieve. It has crippled them.

I have discovered through my own personal experience that Americans teach their children not to express their emotions about little losses. Let a child fall down and scrape a knee and his parent will say, "Oh, get up and stop crying. That didn't hurt. Now quit your crying. Big boys don't cry."

Loss after loss is minimized and unexpressed. When major losses through death or divorce occur, the expression of grief is silenced.

Medical technology has wiped out many childhood diseases, improving longevity markedly. A person at 35 years of age may conceivably never have lost a close family member by death. Add to this the fact that society keeps death in places isolated from us, and you have produced another handicap for grief.

Sudden and violent death has always been with us, but the chance of it occurring is greater now than in the past. Suicide has increased with the drug culture and the break-up of family life. The wide acceptance of dualism with its insistence that a person can continue to live happily apart from the body may tempt teenagers to escape present misery to enjoy instant bliss. Drive-by shootings and random killings plague our society. All of these things and more bring tragic deaths. This means greater difficulty in grief.

Death of the very young or death of the parents of small children is incomprehensible. Survivors in cases like these usually present problems of greater intensity than in cases where the very old die.

The increasing secularization of American society has increased the incidence of unresolved grief. I have not done a scientific study to support this statement, but I have come to this conclusion after working with grieving families for the past few decades as pastor and hospital chaplain.

My observation is that people who have an intimate relationship with God maintain a sense of worth and purpose in life as they pass through experiences of pain, loss and grief.

There well may be a temporary loss of faith, but on the whole there is an easier adjustment on the part of people who have a deep and abiding trust relationship with God.

A faulty concept of God can cause great havoc for the mourner. If God is viewed as an absent landlord who set the world to spinning and walked away, there is no assurance that God takes personal interest in our pain. If we believe that God never lets bad things happen to people who try to live right, we can feel betrayed. Some people have infantile views of God that have never been revised with maturity. Grief can be complicated if we are not willing to take a new look at our concepts of God.

Fortunate is the grieving person who knows God as a Friend. Bringing life into focus after the death of a loved one is a growth experience with God's support.

Strong emphasis on self-reliance and corporate ladder-climbing has produced too many Americans who have too few confidantes. A vertical relationship with God is fine, but we all need horizontal relationships as well, especially in times of crisis. The endless support groups across our country are a sad testimony to the lack of dialogue in the lives of Americans. Trusted friends developed gradually over a period of years remain somewhat permanent. These small, naturally developed circles of support are essential to adjusting to personal loss.

Find the reason why it is difficult for you and determine that you will do something about it.

Helpful Exercises

1. List the customs in your culture and in your family that inhibit your adjustment to loss.

2. Draw a diagram of your support system. List the name and relationship of each person. Circle the names of those who are emotionally the closest to you. Decide whether your support system is adequate. How can you improve it?

3. Look at your list of losses. Select the two losses that were the most problematic. Why were they so difficult for you?

3

Loss - The Broad Spectrum

Writing about loss reminds me of an old farmer who was admitted to the hospital for surgery. He had never been hospitalized before. As he talked about the limitations the physician was setting, he said, "I just don't know how I can part with her, but the doc says she's just too much for me to take care of." Tears were on the old man's face.

My heart went out to him, thinking that he was being forced to place his invalid wife in a long-term care facility. I carefully questioned him about the circumstances and soon discovered that his nearly 500 pound sow had to be sold. The pig's care required lifting heavy buckets and bending over the side of the pen. He could no longer do this. Saying goodbye to the old porker was a major loss.

"You may think I'm a fool to cry over an animal like this," he apologized, "but I've had her for a long time."

The pig was an important part of the farmer's support system. His grief was genuine and to be expected.

Most parents can relate stories about their children and the death of their pets. Real trauma is involved and real grief results.

My granddaughters were two and five when they moved into their new house in the country. Some cold-hearted person dropped three kittens off at the end of their lane. Two of them were claimed by Erin and Jamie. They called to seek my opinion on names for them. They invested hours into caring for their new friends.

Shortly after adopting the kittens they went to visit their friends in Kansas City. During the night a large German Shepherd dog snatched away one of the kittens that managed to crawl out of the garage.

When the girls came home their hearts were broken. For days they carried cat food into the woods and called their kitten's name, but their friend never heard their call.

A couple months after they lost their kitten I visited them. We walked into the woods to search for birds and wildflowers. My job was to record what we saw. We sat on a big log and talked about our discoveries, but the conversation soon turned to the loss of their friend. I could hear the sadness in their little voices.

Loss begins the moment we are born. We lose that warm place beneath mother's heart where we are fed umbilically and rocked amniotically. We emerge into a world of light where we cry to get our food and rocking.

In childhood we lose being at home with parents all day long. Sometimes we are awakened early in the morning and driven to a creepy daycare center where we stand a chance of having little physical contact with a caring person for eight hours.

I stood outside a large church in St. Paul, Minnesota, waiting for the pastor to open the room where I was to present a seminar. Next to the church was a daycare center. I watched dozens of parents delivering their babies and tiny tots to the center. Nearly every child screamed fearfully and clutched at their parent's body and clothes. Their separation anxiety still makes me sad when I drive past daycare centers.

Teenagers lose their identity. They are no longer children, but they are not yet adults. They want to be independent, but they still depend on warm meals and a clean bed to sleep in. They are on an emotional rollercoaster. In their quest for social togetherness they lose many boyfriends and girlfriends. Some of them have been pushed prematurely into dating and have lost their childhood.

People in their twenties lose their parental home. They no longer are foot-loose-and-fancy-free. They have to work to pay the apartment rent.

The middle years come quickly. All the big dreams and achievements are not half realized, but life is more than half over. Loss of dream can be upsetting.

In later years physical and mental deficits appear. Thinking fast and moving fast isn't easy. The chronic diseases of age take their toll.

There are at least three kinds of losses - maturational, situational and accidental.

Maturational loss is felt by the four-year-old when mother brings the new baby home from the hospital. It is sometimes referred to as having your nose out of joint, but to the four-year-old it seems as though the whole body is out of joint.

This is felt by the young bride leaving her parental home. I took my new bride to a honeymoon cabin on the Chesapeake Bay. On the first morning of our marriage I fixed the breakfast. When I called, "Come and get it," there was no response. I went to the bedroom and found her weeping on her pillow. She realized that marriage meant leaving her parental home. Homesickness had descended upon her - grief, if you please.

Maturational loss is not a static experience, it's more of a process. The new bride says goodbye to her parental home when she is old enough to marry. This is followed by losses such as having her own children leave home, selling the big family-sized house, and moving into a one-bedroom apartment designed for "senior citizens." It also includes losses such as the death of a parent or spouse, handicaps due to aging or the inability to drive an automobile.

Situational losses include such things as giving up a pet because of moving to a smaller place in the city, business failure due to economic recession, being fired from a job, and being laid off from work.

Sometimes situational losses are accompanied by secondary losses. For instance, a young man is fired from his job. He learns his lesson and vows to mend his ways on the next job, but due to low seniority, he is laid off from the new job when production slows down. His secondary loss is the shattering of his self-esteem which causes depression to set in.

Accidental losses include things like the sudden and tragic death of a loved one, loss of a limb or bodily function due to a mishap, or the destruction of a home in a tornado.

Losses of all types have a tendency to immobilize the loser, for a short time at least, because the losses do not fit into our scheme of life. Loss is contrary to our expectations.

The divorced people who attend grief support seminars often tell me that they grew up with a dream that they would meet an ideal person for a life companion and that they would always be in love. They pictured their spouses as faithful and totally fulfilled in the marriage. Then one day the horrible story is related - a story of broken vows and shattered dreams.

Divorce doesn't have a place in their expectations. They use denial tactics and entertain false hopes. A lot of energy is spent scheming ways to bring about a reconciliation beyond the point of reason. The loss of a spouse goes against everything they learned to be right and noble.

For some divorced people the word "single" sends chills up and down their spine. They use the word scores of times when referring to others, but they can't handle the use of the word when referring to themselves.

By the time some people attend my support group they have been to a half-dozen counselors looking for somebody to give them a magic formula for mending broken relationships. They may have consumed bottles of tranquilizers and lost many pounds or gained weight from the escape mechanism called "eating," all because their loss was shaped differently than the pattern of life's expectations.

Loss through divorce is devastating, particularly when a person says, "There's something wrong with me. I'm unlovely and incapable of wooing and keeping a mate. I'm doomed to spend the rest of my life alone. Even if somebody else came along I could never trust another person that much again."

Loss seems to inundate those who have no concrete plans for their lives. I heard one person say that everyone needs to have a plan that outlasts life expectancy. Then they need to become excited about the plan and work toward its accomplishment. Without such a plan, a person can be stopped in his tracks when loss occurs.

Another factor that makes loss so overpowering is the absence of a broad support system. People who isolate themselves and form few close friendships have little encouragement in times of loss.

If I'm swimming in deep water I make sure others are swimming with me. My chances of being brought to shore when I lose my endurance are a lot better. I go one step further by making sure I'm among good, strong swimmers.

Loss is an inevitable part of this life. It makes good sense to build into life the kinds of strengths and defenses that maximize the chances of turning losses into gains.

I met a woman who turned her losses into assets. She was a permanent resident of a county home. I was a neophyte pastor with a bundle of "promise texts" in my memory to share with unfortunate people like Mabel.

The charge nurse called up to see if she was ready for company. The answer came back on the intercom - "Eager."

"Oh, I'm so happy you came to see me," she exclaimed. "I've been so eager to show off my beautiful roses. They just put this paper on the walls. I think the roses are absolutely exquisite. With the sun streaming in the windows they make my room look like a rose garden."

I didn't notice the roses on her wall paper. I was distracted by Mabel's blinded eyes. The diabetes had taken its toll.

You'll never know how much it means to me to be in this home," she continued. "Do you know, there are some folks in this place who are too depressed for words. Why, if it wasn't for me they'd have no hope at all. I go around to their rooms every day and cheer them up."

My eyes followed the contour of her body beneath the covers. Just below the hips the covers were flat against the mattress. Mabel had no legs.

The nurse told me that the aides put Mabel in a special chair every day and wheeled her to all the wards. She was known as the angel of the county home.

This inexperienced pastor felt like a pygmy in the presence of a spiritual giant. In spite of her monumental losses, Mabel's assets rose above them.

I'm still trying to discover her secrets. It may be that the discovery can only be made in the presence of loss, but I suspect that Mabel's discovery was integrated into her life long before she went to the county home.

The broad spectrum of loss is not complete until we explore the secondary or abstract losses that are associated with primary losses. Identifying and experiencing these losses fully during acute grief reduces the chances of complicated mourning.

Sometimes secondary losses are called psychological losses. An example is the man who was married to a talented musician. When he attended concerts where she performed, he experienced a great boost to his esteem. After the divorce he no longer experienced that regular boost. Eventually he disliked himself and lost confidence in his ability to form new relationships.

Loss of reputation was a secondary loss for a man who lost his freedom after a fraudulent business deal.

Loss of accomplishment was a secondary loss for a man who retired from his job.

Whether loss is primary or secondary, it can be triggered by many kinds of loss experiences. No loss should be minimized. All loss causes pain.

Helpful Exercises

1. Using your chronological list of losses, place each of your losses under one of the following:

   Maturational loss
   Situational loss
   Accidental loss
   Chronic loss
   Intentional loss

2. Think about your most recent loss. Think about and record the secondary losses accompanying this loss.

4

Coming - Ready or Not

"I don't care how long you know in advance, you're just not ready for it when it happens."

"It hurts even though I had time to do a lot of things I wanted to do."

"She lived a long life and she had a lot of pain. I guess I should be thankful she's at rest, but I hate like everything to say good-bye."

"We both knew it couldn't be much longer. The doctor told us exactly what it was. We talked about it a lot, but I didn't think it would be today."

These are just a few statements I have heard people make right after the death of a loved one.

A business executive at a pre-retirement seminar asked, "Are you ever ready for the death of a person who is very important to you?"

The answer is probably "not completely." The reality is that death is much like the game of "hide and seek" -coming, ready or not.

When people are having a rewarding relationship together, they naturally reach toward the ever fuller development of life's potential. This seems to be a quality that was created into the human race. It was the Creator's plan that people should live forever - continually broadening and enriching every dimension of life.

Death is an enemy that has temporarily interrupted the plan. Despite the reality of death in this life, people usually plan for more living than they can squeeze into their days.

As one man put it who knew his wife was dying, "When the doc told us that Mary had six to nine months to live, we decided right then and there that we'd put six to nine years of living into those six to nine months."

We may not ever be completely ready for a death, but there are some simple concepts that make adjustment much easier when we practice them. Let me share them with you.

1. Let the people you love know who you are.

A man came to see me because he couldn't "get over" his wife's death. As he fought back the tears he said, "I never really showed my feelings to her. She never really knew me. I guess I was very quiet. Oh, she tried to get me to tell her my deep thoughts, but it's always been difficult for me to talk much."

Telling another person who you are is not as easy as it sounds.

I remember reading an article that suggested that when newlyweds fully undress in each other's presence for the first time it is a pledge that they will be transparent and allow themselves to be seen without masking.

Undressing is child's play compared to the monumental task of self-revelation, yet, letting loved ones know you is vital when it comes to adjustment after death.

Heart to heart talks about mutual interests, joys and sorrows can become a regular part of family life. There is no reason why philosophies of life, feelings about pain, sickness and death, and personal preferences about being informed of one's own illness and imminent death cannot be discussed openly.

This openness about every aspect of life will eliminate the game playing and "conspiracy of silence" that occurs during crises in far too many families.

A friend of mine asked me if I could take the time to drive to a distant city to see her parents. Her mother was in the hospital recuperating from a surgical procedure that revealed inoperable cancer. I was to visit with the couple at the hospital.

When I went to the hospital room it was meal time. The husband, I'll call him Jim, had gone to the cafeteria to get a bite to eat. I went to find him, but he wasn't eating. He was sitting in a small lounge in a quiet part of the hospital. After introductions I moved into painful territory.

"Jim, have you and Letha talked about cancer, treatments or the chances of her death?" I asked.

"Not very much," he said with a sigh. "I guess both of us are avoiding it more or less. It's got to be talked about soon. Maybe I'm afraid it wouldn't be good for her to talk about it."

"Maybe it isn't good for her to keep all those feelings on the inside - you too for that matter," I suggested.

"Well, you've got a point there," he said, as he struggled to keep back the tears.

"Perhaps if we all talked together it would be easier," I offered.

At that point Jim nodded, and we walked toward the elevator.

In the room I opened the conversation almost immediately by asking about the surgery and what the physician told them.

Letha jumped at my invitation to talk about it in front of Jim. It was just like a wall of water rushing through a valley after the dam broke. She talked about her frightened feelings and her great sorrow for her husband.

This opened the way for Jim to reminisce about their life together. He shared how unbearable it was to think about Letha's possible death.

Finally the great waves of pain were calming and the two of them were ready to talk about the treatments.

Jim walked me to the front door of the hospital after the visit ended. He took my hand in both of his and said, "Larry, I thank you so much for coming all this way. I can never pay you, but I can tell you that you helped to start a beautiful dialogue between Letha and me. I'm sure that will be reward enough. There is a closeness now that should have been there before. Thank you. Thank you ever so much."

Jim was right. Self disclosure in the family unit should not wait until a crisis is crashing down upon the family members.

2. Come to accept your own value as a person.

This concept is closely related to the first one. Until you feel good about yourself, you will not be comfortable about people knowing who you are.

In an earlier chapter I mentioned that a major loss often causes a lowering of self-esteem. The restoration of self-esteem is much easier when the self-image is strong prior to the loss.

3. Take time to develop the inner person.

A classic example of this concept is the widow of six years who was my solace in times of stress. I was just a young intern-pastor in Ohio, causing many of my own crises due to inexperience and over-confidence. That didn't make a bit of difference to her. She always had a cold drink for me and plenty of time to listen to my woes.

She was more than a good listener, she was interested in so much of life. She was the most widely read person in the church. Any subject I brought up was a great importance to her. She had been developing the inner person for many years. Letters from all over the world were covering half of her dining room table. Needlework projects and handcrafted items adorned her walls.

When her husband died she went through the expected pain and sorrow, but adjustment came quite easily. You see, her interests were uniquely hers and not closely tied to her husband. She was a person in her own right. There was so much within her that could not die with the death of her husband.

4. Learn independence.

Floundering in unfamiliar responsibility that leads to anxiety is a good description of many grieving people who have been overly dependent upon the deceased.

Much of this could be prevented by deliberately learning independence before a major loss occurs.

A surprising number of older men leave the family finances and the food preparation entirely up to the wife. When they are widowed, they become terribly unraveled.

Alex is a good example. I saw him on the front porch of his cottage every day. One day I saw a sign on the porch post that read "Free Kittens." My curiosity won out and I stopped to get acquainted.

Alex's wife died several years before. He was totally dependent on her for everything. His only act of independence was going to work every morning, but now that was mere memory.

Now his daughter was his sole source of support. She cleaned the house, brought in hot meals and took care of all of Alex's financial affairs.

One day the old man made the first independent decision he had made in years - he would start going to church. One problem. His daughter held the purse strings and feared that the old man would get "slap-happy" when the offering plate was passed.

"You go to church and you can make your own meals and clean your own house," she threatened.

Alex never went to church. To my knowledge he never resolved the grief over his wife's death.

With a little more independence he might have picked life up again and brought fulfillment to his later years.

5. Take time to do things together.

A friend of mine promised his wife that they'd go to Florida. His promise was repeated seven years in a row because he was too busy. His wife became ill and died after more than a year of hospitalizations. I can assure you that guilt plagued him for a long time.

Playing together, laughing and leisure time means fewer regrets and easier adjustment after death.

I have observed many people in grief. It seems to me that those who put a lot of living into their days and brought a lot of meaning into the lives of others by way of love, tenderness and expressions of appreciation, are the ones who make easier reentry into life after the loss has been experienced.

6. Develop a realistic set of life-expectations.

Life is not a happy-forever-after situation. We are not immune to sickness, accident, separation and death. Both husband and wife do not necessarily live to be 85 in good health. There may be physical and emotional deficits along the way.

I remember how shocked I was when I began seeing little round spots crossing the windshield as I drove along the highway. I went to an eye doctor who told me I had floaters. He said it was typical of people who are aging. I was horrified. I had always had excellent vision. Floaters never crossed my mind, but when I told my friends about it they laughed. They also had floaters. Why should I be an exception?

A woman was upset when her husband had a stroke. Her husband would never drive again. They planned to travel ten months of the year and spend the other two in a cottage in Colorado. Now she had visions of visiting a nursing home for years to see her husband. She found out that life issues no unconditional guarantees.

Forever bliss is not realistic. Realizing this makes taking some of life's potholes much easier.

7. Put your heart into every day.

Live enthusiastically. Look at the people you live with and appreciate them. As Orville Kelley said, "Make today count." Don't spend much time Monday-morning-quarterbacking the past. Make a solid decision that you'll never judge your past performance by what you think you know today.

8. Learn what to expect.

After conducting classes and workshops on grief for almost two decades, I have had many people tell me that learning what to expect in times of loss definitely helped them cope with their respective losses.

Are you ready for a loss? Not entirely, but being informed about grief prevents some of the surprise and fear.

Helpful Exercises

1. Write out the life expectations that you presently hold to be true. Would any of your expectations pose a problem in the event of a sudden loss? Can you alter those expectations so that they don't pose a problem?

2. Examine your relationship with your closest family member. What parts of that relationship would assist you in adjusting to the loss of that person? What would you like to change? List ways you could go about making the changes.

5

The Anatomy of Grief

I decided to visit the residents in the complex for senior citizens located across from my church. I'm glad I did, particularly because I met Mr. Haskins. He had been working in the kitchen when I rang his doorbell. He showed me to a seat and returned to the kitchen.

"I don't mean to be rude," he called from the kitchen, "but I've got to watch my eggs or else they'll burn. I'm not the best hand at this. Never had to do it before to this extent."

There was a clattering of pans and more talking that I couldn't make out. Finally Mr. Haskins entered the living room carrying a tray with his piping hot lunch. He placed the tray on a small table, pulled a rocking chair up to it and sat down. He bowed his head reverently and soon proceeded to eat.

"You may think it eccentric of me to eat my meal in the living room like this. Maybe you'd understand if I told you that my wife died a short while ago. I sat at the kitchen table with her and ate my meals with her for the last 40 years. Now that she's gone I can't bear to eat in the kitchen. It brings back too many memories. I just won't be the same again," he told me between sobs.

As I listened to Mr. Haskins I realized that his whole life had become out of focus. He had lost his equilibrium. Without his wife there seemed to be no purpose in living another day. He ate, but nothing tasted good. He tried to sleep, but sleep seldom came. During the day he was able to drop off to sleep in his old rocker, but he was awakened by dreams of his wife. He had nobody to talk with. Once in a while the visiting nurse came by, but it was a different one most of the time. The person he related to the best was now gone. Life was so empty.

Thousands of people just like Mr. Haskins are in grief. Some have a pretty good idea of what to expect, but most of them enter grief without prior knowledge of what it is like. They are frightened and sometimes worry about losing their sanity.

If you are having these fears in your time of grief, let me assure you that grief is a normal and healthy reaction to a great loss. It is the attempt of the person to bring about equilibrium - the attempt to be whole again.

There is no stereotype in grief. There is no one way for it to happen. Each person is unique in his makeup and each person grieves in a unique way. God ministers to each person in a unique way.

A woman looked at another woman in a therapy group and said, "I don't think I'll ever get over this. Look at me. I'm falling apart. It's been eight months since John died and I'm just as bad off now as I was the week of his death. But here is Mildred. She lost her husband about the same time I lost mine. Is she suffering? Why, she is miles ahead of me."

The therapist quickly asked the woman if she might not be making an unfair comparison. Further conversation among members of the group revealed that the cases of the two women were entirely different.

In the next few minutes the people in the therapy group built a list of factors that had a bearing on the nature of grief. I'll share that list with you.

The age of the grieving person. Younger people have larger circles of supporting relationships to help in times of loss. Advancing age narrows those circles and limits the opportunities of building new relationships. Age also may have an influence on the general health of the individual. Poor health may hinder recovery from a major loss.

My father wasn't able to adjust to my mother's death. He would look at her picture on the wall and order her to make his meal. His age and physical condition prevented him from reinvesting in life.

The manner of the death. Many people in the group agreed with the woman who lost a son through suicide that this would be the most difficult grief. Sudden and tragic death was considered extremely difficult to cope with. Death of an infant or a young child came very close to the death of a young parent in terms of painful adjustment. Long term illness that leaves a person emaciated or deformed was felt to be extremely difficult for the survivors, particularly if they had a part in the ill person's care resulting in their fatigue prior to the death.

During my hospital chaplain days I saw children in the emergency room who had been run over by a parent. This type of death is so devastating that the lives of parents and grandparents are in jeopardy. I have seen entire families come to a screeching halt.

Previous warning. Some people in the group told about doing much of their grieving before the death, which seemed to lessen the suffering of grief after death. Previous warning didn't seem to help matters if the family and the dying person couldn't bring themselves to talk openly about the imminent death. The lack of openness and intimacy in these cases produced guilt that inhibited the grieving. On the other hand, people who put extra amounts of quality into those last days or weeks were reporting an easier time in their grief.

I worked in hospices for years. I've noticed that families who have lost a loved one less than six months after diagnosis seemed to have a more difficult time in grief. Those who lost approximately two years after diagnosis also seemed to adjust slowly. In the former case there seems to be much denial. In the latter case there are unrealistic expectations arising from numerous rallies after many crises. The best adjustments appeared to take place when loss occurred six to eighteen months after diagnosis.

The personality of the survivor. Some people are very dependent in a relationship. When death occurs they find adjustment too full of responsibilities for which they are not prepared. The independent person may have an easier time adjusting.

Life experiences while growing up. There seemed to be some evidence that people who experienced a number of deprivations in the formative years were better equipped to handle losses of all sorts.

Relationships and interaction with the person who died. A general feeling in the group was that grief went well if the relationship with the person who died went well. People in long-standing grief situations are frequently heard to lament, "If only I could have another chance - just a few more months to show her that I really did love her" or "It wouldn't be so bad if I hadn't hated him so much of the time."

While the nature of grief is different for each person, there are also some fairly common denominators in all grief. I hesitate to call them steps or stages. Perhaps the situation is one of moving from one reaction to another, sometimes with no rhyme nor reason. Here are some of the reactions I have observed in groups I have facilitated.

Confusion. I frequently draw a large circle on the blackboard to represent a grieving person. Inside the circle I draw many arrows pointing in many directions. The arrows represent the many conflicting, painful, upsetting and contradictory emotions. At the top of the circle I write the word CONFUSION.

Shock and numbness. Shock and numbness are very early experiences in grief. Some authors say that shock lasts from two hours to two days, but I have seen people in a dazed condition weeks after the death of a loved one. Trying to recall the activities of the first few weeks after the death may be next to impossible for them.

I remember a thin woman in her eighties sitting in the emergency room family area. The doctor announced very kindly that her husband died. She sat there as if nothing had been said. The doctor told her he was going to return to seeing other patients, but that he would gladly return if she had any questions. For a few moments she flew at the doctor with both fists swinging. Quickly she apologized and returned to her chair. She sat there in silence and shock for over an hour. Her family arrived and led her to a car. She looked like she had been drugged.

Shock may well be a God-given anesthetic that prevents sudden death upon hearing the news of another person's death.

I've seen the same shock in cases of divorce announcements, job losses and broken romances.

Disbelief. A common defense mechanism is stubborn disbelief. Some professionals call it denial. It begins very early in the experience of loss.

A friend of mine went to the hospital to see her father. She didn't know that her father had died. The hospital was unable to reach her because she was in transit to the hospital. She looked through the window of the intensive care unit and saw the family gathered around the bed. The minister was there. Her first impulse was to run out of that hospital so that nobody could tell her. If she wasn't told she wouldn't have to believe it. For her, denial and shock were instantaneous reactions to death.

Fear. Paralyzing fear and dread are reported by many people. Some fear the next event in life. Others fear being alone. The fear of darkness is reported.

Anger. Anger is also prevalent in grief. People are angry at the doctor, the nurse, the hospital, the minister, the person who died, and even at themselves. Anger against God is frequently noticed.

I was traveling in a foreign country a few years ago when I met a teacher who asked me to see his friend when I returned to the United States. His friend, a young mother of three children, had a series of deaths in her immediate family. The latest death was that of her young son. She was terribly angry at God, but the people in her church shamed her for having such feelings. What a relief it was for her to discover that God was just as interested in hearing about her anger as He was her joy. She talked about her anger to me and she talked to God about it. The result - reconciliation with God.

Depression. When denial, anger and extracting promises from God do not change the situation of loss, many people become depressed. This is characterized by feelings of hopelessness, helplessness, despair, resignation, lethargy and intense searching for the missing. Loss of appetite, sleeplessness and disinterest in everything except thoughts of the dead are often noticed. Headaches, backaches, tightening feelings around the chest, feeling that food tastes like sand, inadequate saliva to moisten food, and feelings of nausea are frequently reported. Feelings of exhaustion make it nearly impossible to lift one foot up after the other. Concentration on anything other than the lost love object is unthinkable. Usual abilities to organize things seem to vanish. The term "out of focus" is the best way to summarize it.

Over a period of ten years I asked people in groups to rate themselves on depression symptoms. The results were surprisingly similar from one group to another. Every single group placed sadness at the top of the list. Inability to concentrate and remember was always high on the list along with dislike for pleasures that were appealing prior to the loss.

The emotions and psychosomatic symptoms just described in detail are part of the normal range of reactions to loss through death. Given time and adequate support, the period of acute pain will pass and restored equilibrium will be a believable reality.

Adjustment cannot be charted as a steadily ascending line. There are setbacks along the way. Holidays and anniversaries have a way of causing regression, but the renewed suffering is not nearly as intense as it was earlier.

C.S.Lewis, in his book, A Grief Observed, said, "Grief is like a long valley, a winding valley where any bend may reveal a totally new landscape. Not every bend does. Sometimes the surprise is the opposite one; you are presented with exactly the same sort of country you thought you had left behind miles ago. That is when you wonder whether the valley isn't a circular trench. But is isn't. There are partial recurrences, but the sequence doesn't repeat."

Grief is not to be shunned or escaped. Sooner or later it is experienced. To those who have lost a loved one through death or divorce, or to those who face their own death, I would say, "Let grief happen. It is not an enemy to be silenced. It does not lead to despair, but to growthfulness."

Helpful Exercises

1. On a clean sheet of paper list the feelings you had and continue to have about your most recent loss. Compare them to the reactions mentioned in this chapter.

2. Ask a friend to share his or her feelings and reactions to a major loss. Compare these with your own.

6

Tasks of Grieving

The developing science of thanatology has spawned scores of "how-to" books on grief. Some of them have produced some misconceptions about the components of grief. I read about "phases of grief," "stages of grief," and "steps of grief." Shock, denial, anger, fear, bargaining, depression, and acceptance are commonly mentioned reactions. This systematization of grief is problematic when it gives the misconception that everyone must go through the "phases" one at a time before grieving has really happened.

It is much less problematic to think about the four tasks that are usually accomplished as people move from recent loss to adjustment.

FIRST TASK

The first task is coming to the place where you consider the loss a reality. There is no progress toward regaining your equilibrium until this is done.

One day a young woman who heard about my work walked into my office. Her whole life was a long series of losses. Her latest loss was the death of her teenager. She'd say things like "If Eddie ever died I don't know how I could handle it." I could talk to her about any other loss, but she refused to talk about Eddie. If I pressed her ever so gently, she would say, "I refuse to talk about that. Eddie isn't dead and I won't talk that way."

Sometimes people preserve bedrooms or workshops just as they were the day of the death. They tell themselves that their loved ones are on a trip for a few days. They cannot perform the next tasks of grieving until they have said, "I know he is dead and won't be coming back."

At the close of a therapy session a woman said, "You know, I think I am finally beginning to heal."

"How can you tell?" I asked.

"My husband died two months ago in the Brighton hospital. Every day since then I have called the head nurse on the cancer floor and asked how Barney is doing. Every day the nurse quietly reminded me that Barney had died. But I didn't call the hospital once this week. I know Barney died. I believe it now. That's why I can tell that I am beginning to heal."

SECOND TASK

The second task of grief is to be willing to experience the pain and suffering caused by a major disruption in life.

Nobody gets excited about pain. It is almost instinctive to withdraw from anything that is accompanied by discomfort. People in grief are no exception.

As I work with groups of grief stricken people, I can be ever so gentle, yet some will hesitate to attend the second session because of the pain. A few even say that the group meeting caused them to have a regression.

I am discovering that people who make these objections usually have avoided all thoughts, situations and sights that would cause the slightest pain. When they attend a group meeting where people are sharing the nature of their losses and where painful feelings are expressed, it sends their own painful feelings cascading into the consciousness of the mind. Then they feel a strong urge to run from the pain.

Pain must be experienced if healing is to occur. Pain must be expressed if growth and new life are to result.

I have frequently observed small children receiving an injury, physical or emotional, when the parents were not around. They show the hurt for a few minutes, but fight back the tears. Then a parent arrives on the scene. The child runs to the parent and breaks down in tears. They finally express the pain experienced earlier. What relief. What healing.

In grief, pain is a sign of healing. Feeling and expressing pain is healthy and absolutely essential.

My friends who work with people who have suffered major losses agree that when people can't or won't experience and express pain, they become stalemated. Progress toward recovery is halted.

Going through pain has a way of mellowing the pain. The sharp sting is lessened. Eventually thoughts of the lost evoke mostly good and warm memories. Now the person is ready for the third task of grief.

THIRD TASK

The third task of grief is to move back into the familiar environment associated with the person who is now gone.

A friend of mine worked in the same establishment where her husband worked. After he had divorced her, she was devastated with pain every day she went to work. It was not until she had freely expressed and worked through her pain that she could walk into her place of employment with her head held high.

Some people travel, work a second job, or stay with friends and relatives to avoid going home after the loss of a spouse or child. Young people may leave home or run the streets to avoid going home to a house where a loved one is missing.

All of us move back into familiar environments differently. Some do it gradually and some do it abruptly. The important thing is to do the tasks without getting bogged down.

A friend of mine was comfortable in the home where she and her husband had lived together, but she couldn't look out the window at the fruit trees her husband had planted before his death. She often screamed as she walked from the car to the house. The orchard was an acutely painful part of her surroundings long after she had adjusted to other aspects of her loss.

She finally took a memory trip through the history of the orchard as it related to her husband. She wrote about the orchard in her journal and talked about it to friends. Eventually she was able to walk among the trees, touch the boughs with her hands, and talk aloud about the part her husband played in the planting of the trees. Within weeks she was able to enjoy walking in the orchard.

If you discover a part of your world that causes pain, don't permit this to discourage you. The pace of adjustment is not all that important. The key to recovery is actively grieving as soon as possible.

FOURTH TASK

The fourth task is saying good-bye. This is the slow process of withdrawing the mountains of emotional energy invested in the lost relationship and reinvesting that energy in other relationships.

Some people call this psychological amputation. Perhaps this is their way of saying that "letting go" or "saying good-bye" to a loved one is a major shock to the system. On the other hand, amputation is sometimes the only way to save a person's life. This is true in grief. The only way you can be free to go on living in a satisfying manner is to say good-bye to the relationship that can no longer be.

Scores of people who attend support groups report that they had to say good-bye before they really began to live again. This is not to say that they discarded their memories. Memories are symbols of love. Saying good-bye is admitting and acting on the fact that a present relationship with a lost person cannot be productive. It is accepting the fact that living in the past is cheating you and others who could benefit from your fellowship.

You do not withdraw all the emotional energy in a lost relationship. Instead you keep a small investment in memories of the person you lost. Now you relate to that person as missing, not alive as before. You can reminisce and talk about him or her with pleasure. And this new type of emotional attachment does not keep you from forming other friendships. Once again you can engage in a variety of life pursuits.

Helpful Exercises

1. Choose several losses from your chronological list of losses. Write out how you accomplished the four tasks for each loss. If there are any unfinished tasks, list ways you can do them.

2. Think about a loss in your family to which satisfactory adjustment was made. Try to identify ways in which each of the four tasks were completed.

3—G.R.

7

Moving Toward Recovery

When a person goes through grief, he or she is caught between the need to suffer pain and the urge to run.

The sooner and the more intensely the person experiences suffering, the sooner he recovers. I must qualify that statement however. When a person experiences great change in life through death or divorce and then suffers pain in coming to terms with the change, there can be either growth or devastation as a result. When change and pain are accompanied by the support of meaningfully-related people, there is growth. Deprived of support, a person can become very bitter.

For this reason a grieving person should be encouraged to reach out to others and to lean on friends and professional helpers.

Running puts off the experience of pain to a later time. Ways of running are legion. Drink, drugs, travel, work, promiscuity, wreckless sports, and pleasure extravaganzas are just a few. The tragedy of running is the devastation and heartache that so often occur. Ultimately a person must go through the pain in order to be healed. How much better it is to let the pain happen early in grief.

I will suggest four steps that are certain to move you toward recovery:

1. Think.

This may be the opposite of some of the advice given to you. Frequently people are told, "Just put it out of your mind. Don't think about it. Stay away from the place where he had lived. Don't go near the cemetery where you are forced to think about him."

I would encourage you to be unafraid of your thoughts. Let them happen. For instance, if you drive by the restaurant where you had dinner with the person, relive the entire evening in your mind. Recall the menu, the conversation, how he was dressed, and the ride home.

If you live in the house where the person had resided before death, go from room to room and rethink all of the events connected with each room. The room where you had eaten your first meal after the honeymoon, the room where you had listened to your favorite music, the room where the children were conceived, the room where you last kissed - take a memory trip through familiar places.

The thinking process helps us to accept the reality of the loss both intellectually and emotionally. Intellectual acceptance comes easily, but emotional acceptance doesn't come until some months after the loss.

In driver's education we learn that there is some distance between the time when we apply the brakes and the time when the car stops. The application of death or divorce news may register in the head almost immediately, but the registering in the heart, like the full stopping of the car, is some time away.

The thinking process facilitates acceptance.

2. Write.

You can think thirty years in three minutes, but it takes longer to write it. That's why I suggest that grieving people keep a journal during their grief. Write down all the details, but also the feelings you have. Tell your journal how life is different without the person you lost. Tell about the things that help and the things that hurt. Analyze your anger, your loneliness, and your frustration. Be very open with your journal. This slows down your thinking and tends to lessen the pain that accompanied your first thoughts.

3. Talk.

Talk to people who are willing to listen without feeling they need to say something. Choose a person who isn't judgmental.

Have a certain progression to your talking. Starting with the immediate loss, talk about details and feelings concerning events all the way back to the first time you met the person who died. If the relationship with the person you are talking to permits, talk about all the relationships with other people prior to your meeting the person who died. Reviewing meaningful relationships prior to meeting the deceased will help you to accept the possibility of having meaningful relationships after the death.

Talking is a process whereby you gradually experience a lessening of the acute pain of separation. You begin to say good-bye, to psychologically emancipate yourself from the bondage you willingly formed with the person who died.

Gradually change the thrust of your conversation to yourself and your future, but first of all, be sure you have spoken about your grief feelings as extensively as you need to.

4. Weep.

Weeping is a God-given release when we are going through a time of stress. Do not choke back the tears. Let them flow. Crying is not an indication of a weakened faith. The New Testament indicates that Jesus wept. Why shouldn't we?

I spoke to a group of 35 Methodist women about grief. All of them were weeping at the same time. I commented, "I'm happy to see that all of you are healthy." They were amused at my comment, but I was really serious. Weeping during grief is healthy.

Dr. James Peterson of the University of Southern California says, "No one cries very much unless something of real worth is lost. So grieving is a celebration of the depth of the union. Tears are the jewels of remembrance - sad, but glistening with the beauty of the past." ("On Being Alone" The Adventist Chaplain, Nov. 1975, Glendale, CA p.5)

The four steps are in no way seen as a magic cure. They are simply facilitators of the grief process. Grief is not resolved in a hurry. Most people want to know how long grief lasts, but there is no way of putting a time on it. Some authors say that acute grief lasts 6 to 8 months. Don't count on it. Instead of keeping track of the months, look for subtle improvements. Rejoice over each small advancement. You'll take a few steps backward, but that's to be expected. As long as you keep your eyes on the goal, you'll do fine.

Speaking of healing, C.S.Lewis said, "There was no sudden, striking, and emotional transition. Like the warming of a room or the coming of daylight, when you first notice them they have already been going on for some time." (A Grief Observed, The Seabury Press, 1963, p. 49)

As I write this chapter I look back over 18 years of conducting bereavement support groups. I recommended the four steps to each group because they really help to resolve the difficult issues every grieving person faces. A person in grief is often in a listless state and can spend months doing nothing to adjust. Such a person may feel very much out of control, but these steps restore a sense of being in control.

I have observed that feelings of anxiety are less when people have some choices in how grief proceeds. That's why I tell them to set a time each day for thinking, writing, talking, and crying. This deliberate grieving reduces the times of breaking down in public.

If you avoid active grief, you may think you are handling your loss, but there may be little forward motion. You have to go through the pain produced by these four steps if you want to adjust to your loss.

Helpful Exercises

1. Consider your most recent loss or a loss you have not resolved. Follow the four steps described in this chapter. Dedicate time for this each day. Continue for six weeks or until the pain is noticeably mellowed.

2. Review your journal entries on previous days of the above exercise. Make notes in the journal about any positive changes you notice.

3. You might want to help a person grieving the same loss to take these four steps. Reaching out to others is very therapeutic.

8

Review and Reconstruction

Frequently I am with families in the emergency room when the physician announces the death of a loved one. The reactions vary. The usual response is stabbing pain followed by tears. Within minutes a numbing effect takes over. Sometimes short periods of rage appear, but regardless, disbelief settles in. Even after seeing the body, the family walk to their cars saying, "I just can't believe it. This can't be happening to us."

The funeral is usually a blur. The family knows there were many people there, but they can't remember names. The minister's remarks are seldom remembered. The whole episode seems like a bad dream.

Soon after the funeral many people go in search of the person who died. They look for the lost in crowds, at church, on subways and at home. They pine and yearn for the person to be there as usual.

A friend of mine was completing a house that he and his wife started to build just before she died. Seven months after her death he said to me, "I have never admitted this to a soul, but I really do believe that when I move into that house she'll be there."

A woman told me that she fully expects to see her husband in his usual chair when she gets home from grocery shopping. When he isn't there she goes about the house calling his name. He never answers. After the letdown she curls up on the bed and cries.

These are not unusual behaviors. Intellectually the reality has registered to some degree. On all other levels the person still lives with the loved one.

In early grief a person strives to keep the relationship alive. Great efforts are made to retain the sense of presence, but underlying these efforts is the sad awareness that all efforts are futile.

In my early work with grieving people I urged them to say goodbye to their relationship with the lost. Many of these people resisted my suggestion because they were still searching for the person who was missing. They were putting all their energy into preserving the relationship - the opposite of what I was asking them to do.

Pamela came to my office on several occasions. She listened to me saying, "Pamela, it might be helpful if you could say goodbye to your relationship with Jack. You are trying to hold onto someone who is no longer able to meet your needs."

One day she turned to me and screamed, "I don't want to say good-bye to Jack. Can't you understand? I want him with me and you won't take him away from me."

Pamela and many other grieving friends of mine have concluded that it's better to cooperate with the early need to cling to the relationship than to resist it.

They discovered that reviewing and reconstructing the total relationship has a comforting quality. Not only is it comforting, it also gets the expression of feelings started. This wards off getting stuck midstream in grief.

As people share their recollections of a relationship with me, they'll sometimes stare out the window. With a smile on their faces they'll say something like, "I'll never forget how happy we were when we were married. Ben was full of life. So handsome. And I was so proud to be in his arms."

Sometimes there is laughter as we review a part of the relationship. The laughter relaxes tense muscles. Laughter is also a way of expressing sorrow when tears do not come easily.

After weeks of thinking, journaling and talking about her husband, a woman had an amazing breakthrough. It happened after an hour of reminiscing and laughing about the humorous qualities of their relationship. For the first time since her husband died, she was smiling. That smile went to the very depths of her soul. She said to herself, "Ah, I can feel well again. This is a sign that I'll find life worth living even though my husband died. This must be an evidence of healing."

This is exactly what I wanted her to discover in her early grief. The discovery took place by following her natural attempts to keep the relationship alive. By early review and reconstruction, she moved to a point where she was ready to begin saying good-bye. That couldn't happen until she had a small promise of healing on the horizon.

Hospital staff need to see the important role they play in this process. They are often with people at the time of death. A physician, nurse, social worker or chaplain can encourage the newly bereaved family to tell the story of the person's life. Reviewing can begin immediately if hospital staff will take time to be with the family.

When a loved one dies, the bereaved person wants to share with another person how worthwhile the loved one was. When that opportunity is not provided, there is an empty feeling inside. A choked up sensation takes over, making future sharing of feelings difficult.

Reviewing and reconstructing the relationship becomes repetitive. People say to me, "I must sound like a broken record. Aren't you bored with this?"

I am very quick to let them know that the repetition is vital. How I feel isn't important. What the repetition is doing for them is what really matters.

Grieving people must find a tolerant and non-judgmental friend who will listen patiently. They need people who will share their story many times.

People who don't understand the value of reviewing say things like, "You've got to quit going over the same thing again and again. It's not doing you a bit of good." But it is doing good.

Frequently reviewing the relationship will bring some unpleasant things to the surface. This is a necessary part of therapy.

A widow was talking about how protective her husband was. He cared for everything. She didn't even know how to write a check. She suddenly blurted out, "Why didn't Danny teach me some of these things? He babied me too much. Maybe if he hadn't made me so dependent, I could handle being alone."

A divorced man told his story for the fifth time. He said, "She was always so passive. I wish she had spoken up and told me what was eating at her, then I could have done something to change. Now I know what I needed to change, but she won't give me a chance."

Talking about the negative parts of the relationship provides a chance to admit anger and analyze it constructively. Admission of guilt also takes place. Once these feeling are confronted they can be analyzed and resolved.

Part of the relationship that needs to be verbalized is the series of events that led up to the death and the death itself. In the case of divorce, the series of events leading up to the separation needs to be put into words. These painful events can be locked in the mind and never be discussed. This is a mistake. Reviewing these events with others mellows the pain.

Any part of the relationship that a person wishes to avoid should be reviewed and reconstructed deliberately. The longer avoidance is practiced, the more difficult adjustment will be.

One of my favorite ways of helping a grieving person is to sit back in my chair and say, "John must have been a unique person in your life. Tell me about him." Then I listen as long as the person cares to talk.

Scores of people finish a session like this by saying, "I feel so much better now that I've talked about him. I guess I needed to do it."

Separation from a loved one is unnatural to the mind. The cutting short of a relationship may be irreversible, but the lingering afterglow need not be denied. Totally experiencing that warmth is both comforting and preparatory to recovery.

Don't force yourself to review and reconstruct the entire relationship in one sitting. You'll tire yourself. Too much at one time may produce anxiety. Go about it slowly. Give yourself weeks or months to cover the relationship in depth.

Some days you may feel like taking a break from thinking about the past. You probably need a respite from the pain. Go ahead and occupy yourself with diversionary activity. After all, emotions are similar to the muscles of your body. Both are meant to be relaxed periodically.

As you reminisce over the past you will gradually admit to yourself that experiences with the person will not happen again. Slowly you will sense the need to bid farewell to what cannot be.

Helpful Exercises

1. Review and reconstruct the entire relationship with an important person you lost. Methodically think through the good, the mediocre, and the bad aspects of the relationship.

2. Review the plans you had for the future. Reflect on the part the missing person had in those plans. Spend some time constructing tentative plans that don't include the person you lost.

9

Saying Good-bye

My decision to leave home at sixteen to attend private school was exciting. The lure of the big city made me eager to be on my way. I loaded my foot locker into the trunk of the 1942 Studebaker. My father made sure the barnyard gate was closed and then he climbed behind the wheel. As we drove down the lane, strange feelings began to churn inside. The feelings became stronger as we carried the footlocker into the rooming house in downtown Philadelphia. It was all so foreign to me.

In the school parking lot I bid my parents farewell. My mother hugged me for the first time that I could remember. My father awkwardly hugged me. The only other physical contacts with my father were an occasional good-natured slap on the knee as we worked together and an occasional spanking.

They drove out of the parking lot. There I stood - all alone in a new world. The confusing feelings that had built up during the three-hour trip suddenly burned their way to my tear ducts. I fought the tears back, but to no avail. The old Studebaker looked blurred as it disappeared down Drexel Road. The lump in my throat was so big that I feared choking.

I walked around the corner of the school where nobody could see me. There I regained my composure before facing my new school family.

Saying good-bye was the most painful experience of my life up to that time. Even though I would have both of my parents for thirty years more, that first good-bye was a shattering experience.

With the passsing of years I have had to say good-bye to relationships that were terminated by death. The pain of knowing that there would be no more reunions in this life nearly paralyzed me. Many times I wondered how I could go on, but I did go on. I did say good-bye. I did find healing.

I learned how to say good-bye from the scores of grieving people who have come into my life in the last twenty-five years. I'll share their secrets in this chapter.

Reviewing and reconstructing the relationship in thought, journaling and conversation is essential to saying good-bye. Celebration of relationship precedes termination of relationship.

When I tell people they need to say good-bye, they cringe because they misunderstand.

I don't advocate saying good-bye to memories. Memories are

the priceless gems securely encased in the mind.

I conducted a seminar for sixteen people. The average age was 82.

Ella stood out in bold relief. She was 86. She began telling her story.

"My dear husband died in this very hospital just two weeks ago," she said in a quivering voice. "I can't tell you what a blow it has been to me."

Struggling with tears she continued. "But I've got to get hold of myself. I've got to put him out of my mind. I can't think about him. I've got to try not to think about him."

"Ella, who told you not to think about your husband?"

"My minister and my doctor. They said it wouldn't be good for me."

"Ella, do you have any children?" I asked.

"Yes, sir. I have two sons," she informed me proudly.

"Do you remember when your oldest son went to school the first day?"

"Yes."

"Now, Ella, I want you to pretend. Pretend that you're standing at the front door of your house on that first school day. You stoop down and say, 'Willie, when you go past old Mr. York's cherry tree, don't you dare think about red-eyed elephants in the cherry tree.' You tell him that three times before he leaves the house. You warn him again as he leaves the front yard."

"Now tell me, Ella. What is Willie going to think about when he passes Mr. York's cherry tree?"

A slight twinkle came into her eyes as she said, "Why, the red-eyed elephants, of course."

"And when they told you not to think about your husband, what did you think about?" I asked.

"My husband. After all, we lived together for nearly 60 years. How could I not think about him?" she responded.

"Ella, you have my permission to go back over your wonderful memories of your husband. I'd love to hear about how you met him. I like romance stories. Could you share with me?" I eagerly asked.

That was just the invitation she needed. For twenty minutes Ella shared her memories with us. At certain points she was laughing through her tears.

She finally gave a loud sigh and exclaimed, "Oh, I feel so much better now. I wish somebody had told me two weeks ago that it was alright to remember."

Memories are painful at first, but with adjustment they are monuments to the worthwhileness of that person's life.

I don't ask a grieving individual to say good-bye to the person. The unique character and personality of the loved one is integrally woven into the life-fabric of the person who grieves. To say good-bye to the person would require removing many elements of one's lifestyle that are irreversibly stamped by the influence of the person.

Parents who lose a child and try to say good-bye to that person are in for painful surprises. One day they may hear or see the identical expressions and mannerisms of the dead child in one of their living children.

I have met parents who avoided a living child because he or she reminded them of the child who died.

Saying good-bye to the person is not realistic - to say the least.

Saying good-bye to hopes of meeting the person who died is never encouraged. In my experience with grieving people I have concluded that this hope facilitates the desired recovery. When a person has no hope of ever seeing his or her loved one again, the journey toward adjustment is much rockier.

To rip that hope away from a person is inexcusable. Therapists who insist that a grieving person say good-bye "forever" or that he or she will "never" see the loved one again are not wise.

A clinical psychologist friend of mine came to be with me in a time of loss. He put his hand on my shoulder, looked into my eyes and said, "Larry, now what do you think of the scant empirical studies that suggest faith doesn't really make a difference?"

My response was immediate. "I think they need to do more thorough research."

"I agree with you one hundred percent," he replied. I knew by his tone of voice that hope had guided him through a deep loss.

If I don't ask people to say good-bye to memories, the person, or their hopes of future reunion, what do I encourage them to say good-bye to? I encourage them to say good-bye to the relationship as it once existed but can no longer exist in this lifetime.

When a grieving person reaches out to a relationship that has ceased, the absence of response is frustrating. Human needs, once met by that relationship, are no longer met. Anxiety mounts. Loneliness deepens. Depression settles in.

These unpleasant experiences could last over a long period. They could cause you to get stuck in grief. To prevent this I suggest saying good-bye to the relationship in bits and pieces.

If a person has already reviewed and reconstructed the relationship earlier, it's simply a matter of arranging the parts of the relationship from least important to most important. Begin saying good-bye to the part that is least important and move to the most important parts.

I suggest saying good-bye aloud to the person who was lost. Vocalizing the good-bye adds definiteness to what you are doing. Addressing the missing person is very logical. You may intellectually accept the reality of loss, but you don't accept it on other levels. For all practical purposes that missing person still lives with you. Addressing the missing person brings acceptance on all levels.

Some people can review a part of the relationship and say good-bye audibly, others find it easier to write the good-bye first and then read it aloud. Each person must find a way that is best for him or her.

I will share a few cases that illustrate this process.

Barbara lost her husband in a freak accident. Over a year later she was depressed and unable to care for her family.

My sessions with her were so painful that she often left the room and refused to return. Eventually she reviewed and reconstructed her relationship during our sessions.

Day after day she wrote good-bye to parts of the relationship and read them aloud. After covering every part of the relationship she felt it important to say a general good-bye.

Her friend called me to say that Barbara was hysterical, so I went to see her. She was sitting in a chair with a listless expression on her face. She was exhausted. In her hand she held her journal.

"I said my final good-bye," she said quietly.

She looked up at me. A faint smile broke out on her face. "Do you want me to read it to you?"

"Barbara, I'm so happy for your progress. Please read it," I urged.

"Oh, my God, Johnnie - you are dead. You are dead. I will never see you again in this life. Until that day when we meet again, good-bye Johnnie. Good-bye Johnnie. I love you. You know, God, I don't know you very well, but when I get things straightened out I'd like to get to know you better. OK?"

Barbara leaned her head back against the cushion and cried. After the tears stopped she sighed and quietly said, "I'm glad I'm finally finished."

The next day she went shopping for groceries and cleaned the house thoroughly. She cooked the first good meal in many months. After the meal was over, she gathered her three children close to her. "Children," she lovingly said, "your Momma has spent the last year living for herself. Now I'm going to live for you. Together we're going to be happy again."

A week later Barbara, who had once been very angry at God, asked, "Larry, have you a Bible I can use? Maybe you can tell me where to read to get to know God."

Margie's husband died suddenly during an athletic event. Months later she was harvesting corn in the garden. It suddenly struck her that she and Ed had planted that corn together in the spring.

She reviewed the entire experience in her mind. Going to the store for the seeds and fertilizer, planting the long rows, covering the seeds and finally hoeing the weeds - all of this was reviewed.

Right there in the garden Margie looked up at the blue sky. With hot tears running down her cheeks she cried, "Ed, Honey! Ed, my dear! You and I planted this corn in the springtime, but we'll never plant corn again in this life. Good-bye to planting corn in the springtime. Good-bye, Ed, to planting corn in the springtime."

Margie told me, "I stood in that corn field and cried for a good half an hour. When I was all through crying, I felt a little space inside of me for something other than constant thoughts of Ed. I had a new freedom that I hadn't felt since before Ed died."

Margie continued saying good-bye until she was ready to move away from her grief entirely. There will be some parts of the relationship that she will need to say good-bye to several times before the pain mellows. This is especially true of the most intimate parts of the relationship.

If peace and healing don't come after a few good-byes to a given part of the relationship, be persistent in saying good-bye until the acute pain eases. It will ease.

Saying good-bye is painful. You will find a hundred reasons not to do it. Do not give in to your reasons. Begin saying good—bye even when you don't want to.

This is the part of grieving that most people resist adamantly. Resistance hinders healing.

Begin saying good-bye. Until you do, you'll be unable to say hello to new relationships with God or people.

Say good-bye. Then say hello to a new chapter of your life. You may not like the chapter you write, but ultimately you'll look back and see some meaning in what your life has written.

Helpful Exercises

1. Think of one activity you engaged in with a person who is missing. Write a farewell to doing it. Read the farewell aloud. Say the farewell from the heart. Say it repeatedly until the tears subside and the pain softens.

2. Review the ways in which you said farewell in past loss situations.

10

The Broken Circle

Carefully I drew a circle on the blackboard. I drew a second circle partially overlapping the first. Then I erased one of the circles, leaving one circle with a piece missing. I turned to the group of grieving people and asked, "Can anyone interpret what I just did?"

"Sure can," came the response from a woman who was recently divorced. "Once I shared my life with another person, but he left me. Now there's a big part of my life missing."

Her answer prompted others in the group to share their interpretations. The ideas were so fascinating that I decided to continue drawing the diagram for Grief Recovery groups. Over the years I've heard dozens of responses. I'll share a few with you.

A Perception Problem

When you have a deep relationship with another person and then lose that relationship, it feels like you're not a whole person. You really are whole. You're still the same person with the same qualities and potential for living a productive life. It's just that the great loss leaves you with a perception problem. After you assess your assets and personal qualities, you'll begin to see things you couldn't see before. As you talk to friends about your perception problem they will help you understand that you didn't lose a part of yourself. You lost the relationship with an important person.

A Part Of You Is Missing

The crescent shaped piece taken out of the circle represents the part of you that you invested in the person you loved. That's why you feel so empty when a loved one dies or divorces you. You never recover that part of you. You may fill that empty space with other relationships and interests, but there will always be spaces that can't be filled. It's like filling a square space with round pieces of wood. There will always be little empty spaces.

Scars Will Last

You can fill that empty space over a long period of time. Relationships of different kinds will once again meet your needs. Compare it to surgically removing a piece of skin and flesh. Eventually your body will fill in the space, but there'll always be a scar to remind you of the excision.

Something Left

Of course there is something missing when a loved one dies or divorces you, but did you ever stop to think that there is still something left? You are not totally bereft. The fact that there is so much left to work with means there is still a purpose for your life. If you keep looking at the missing part, you won't have time or energy to utilize the part remaining. Crying with a broken heart over what is lost is necessary. Just remember that there comes a time to reorganize and use the remainder.

A Life Imprint

Looking at that remaining circle can tell you about the imprint the other person's life made upon yours. The design of your life has been changed. Your priorities have been rearranged. In some ways you'll always be different because that special person merged his or her life with yours.

It Comes From Within

That altered circle tells you that you aren't the same after a loss, but you can become whole in spite of the changes. That dent in the circle can move out to form a perfect circle again, but the outward movement toward wholeness must come from within. It has a lot to do with your attitudes and your outlook on life. The initiative comes from within you.

Months may need to go by before the inner strength is sufficient to complete that circle, but it can be done by the proper forces within.

I Haven't Lost Anything Of Myself

Maybe the drawing of circles and the erasure improperly pictures what happens in relationship and loss of relationships. Maybe you should picture it as the overlapping of two pieces of cloth. The overlapping parts are sewn together. Instead of erasing, you should represent the loss by cutting off the part of the one circle that does not overlap the other.

This would tell you that your life is permanently strengthened by your relationship with the person you love. What you gave in the relationship was not lost because love does not diminish with the giving. The love of the person who is now gone is still a part of your life. You are richer for having shared life with that special person.

You Are So Vulnerable

Just when I thought I had heard all the possible responses to my circle drawing, I met a woman who came up with a new one.

"If I were erasing that one circle, I'd erase the entire circle. The remaining part of the second circle would look like a large letter C.

"When my husband died I felt open to the world. I felt vulnerable and insecure. I was afraid. The person who had been there to protect me was no longer there. There was nobody to care for me now. That large, gaping hole allows many things to come against me, but my defenses are too weak to ward them off.

"It's going to take a long time to close that gaping hole."

Your Turn

As you read each interpretation you may have disagreed with parts of all of them. Your disagreement may mean that you are at an altogether different milestone in recovery. You could profit from writing your own interpretation once a month for the next year.

As I listen to people discussing the circle diagram I realize that most grieving people are struggling to rebuild shattered self-esteem. They are grappling with the shaping of a new identity. The strengthening of self-esteem and identity seems to bring a more positive interpretation of the diagram.

Some of the interpretations reflect the crucial beginnings of reorganization. Others show form nearing completion.

In most cases, the grieving people I have met became creatures of greater beauty for having gone through the pain of loss. Deeper substance of character is present. They developed a broader sense of their own value as children of God.

An Exercise

I watch charming and talented people in my groups collapse into a heap of perceived worthlessness. At times I want to take them by the shoulders and shake them. Of course, that would only complicate matters. Instead I devised an exercise designed to restore their self-confidence.

At the top of a paper I ask them to write I AM VERY SPECIAL. I ask them to list all their good qualities on one side of the page. If they find it difficult, I ask them to seek the assistance of a good friend. When they bring the list to the group I ask everyone to add their impressions to the list. Then we celebrate their good qualities in the group.

I ask everyone to practice affirmation. Frequently we make comments like "Jim, you are really kind." "I think you have a lot of wisdom, Mary." "There's a warmth about you, Linda, that always gives us a lift." "I'm so happy that you are in this group. You make it easier for me to feel safe."

The final part of the exercse is building a set of goals based upon the good qualities. My favorite memory is of an artistic woman who set a short term goal of taking a refresher course in oil painting. Her long term goal was to teach the course at the art center. She was well on her way to repairing the broken circle.

Helpful Exercises

1. Apply the circle-drawing to your own situation of loss.

2. Write down your assets as suggested in this chapter and be sure to construct short range and long range plans. Indicate how you will carry out the plans.

3. Ask a friend to review your personal assets. Invite him or her to suggest personal traits and abilities that you have not listed.

11

Grief and Marriage

Jack and Cindy stood at a crossroad in their marriage. Cindy moved out of the house when Jack was out of town on business. After weeks of negotiating, Jack convinced her to come home, but they knew they needed help to save their marriage.

The marriage counselor had enough insight to take a loss history before the sessions began. The history uncovered the cause of the trouble. Five years earlier Jack and Cindy welcomed their firstborn into the world, but the cherished baby died a few hours after birth.

Jack came from a family who took pride in being "strong" in a crisis. The expression of feelings was considered "weak" and "letting down the family tradition."

Cindy came from a warm and expressive family. They did a lot of touching and hugging. When something disturbed Cindy she talked about it freely.

When the baby died, Jack locked his feelings deep inside. He bottled them up. He refused to listen to Cindy when she needed to talk about her sad feelings. His philosophy was "avoid it and it will eventually go away."

Cindy needed tenderness from Jack. She wanted to cry and talk in his arms, but his arms were not open to her. She took daily walks through the fields and forests of their farm. She wept and talked to the wild flowers and the birds. The longer she wept to the daisies and the red-winged blackbirds, the deeper grew her resentment toward Jack.

The deeper Jack buried his pain, the more enraged he felt within. In moments of fatigue and provocation he became physically abusive to Cindy.

After 5 years of this behavior, both Jack and Cindy chalked up their marriage impasse to other factors. The counselor helped them identify the primary cause of their rocky relationship - the inability to grieve together.

Husbands and wives share scores of activities, ideals, interests, and dreams. They share the intimate and sacred moment of conception. They celebrate birthdays and wedding anniversaries. Events of little significance to others may be highlights for two people in love. But death is different. Sharing and supporting during grief is often missing. The unwillingness to share openly is misunderstood. Disappointment turns to resentment. Resentment becomes full-blown anger. The marriage reels under the blows of distrust.

Every level of marriage is touched by grief. Let's look at those levels.

The Spiritual Level

Personal friendship with God is the bedrock of a strong marriage. God is the source of love. When a person's friendship with God is faltering, the flow of love into that person's life is unsteady. The flow of love into the marriage is not adequate.

The loss of a loved one is frequently followed by a loss of faith. The awareness of God's love and interest grows dim. Feelings of being rejected by God lead a person to cry out, "Oh, God, why have you deserted me?"

It's frightening to hear your spouse say, "I can't pray anymore. As far as I'm concerned, I'm not interested in God at all. He let me down. I'm through with Him."

Both husband and wife may experience a loss of faith at the same time. This is not indicative of a deliberate spiritual lapse. Deep feelings of abandonment are usually the cause.

Preaching and remonstrating deepen the feelings of rejection. Loyalty, love and support shorten the loss of faith.

When a grieving person feels cut off from God, the gap is often bridged by a person who is not afraid to enter the pain of that person.

I spoke to a group of people who had cancer. A man in his fifties shared his story with the group. I'll call him Mr. Howell.

Mr. Howell's doctor came into the hospital room and announced that the diagnosis of cancer was clearly confirmed. The disease had metastasized to many parts of his body. The prognosis was very poor.

Mr. Howell was so angry inside that he could barely contain himself. He was angry at God. He felt abandoned by God and wanted nothing more to do with him. When his family left that evening he turned off his light, turned his face toward the wall and wept out his anger.

At that point a nurse came to the doorway of his room. "Mr. Howell, are you alright?" she said.

"Yes," he answerd sharply.

"Are you crying?" she asked.

"No," he yelled angrily.

Now, that nurse could have turned on her heels and left Mr. Howell to suffer alone, but she didn't. She came into his room and sat down at the head of the bed. She held Mr. Howell's hand and stroked his hair.

"It's OK to cry, Mr. Howell, when you think you are going to die before you thought. We nurses cry, too, when our patients aren't doing well. It's OK to be angry. We nurses are angry too when our patients are dying. If you want me to, I'll stay right here. I'll listen as long as you need to talk."

Then Mr. Howell made a profound statement to that group. "I knew that the lady in a white uniform was a nurse, but she really wasn't a nurse. God was sitting by my bed. He was assuring me that even though I felt forsaken and lonely, He was still with me."

Mr. Howell discovered that faith can be restored when a friend is willing to be present in a non-judgmental way. His spiritual perception was cleared up by the human demonstration of God's love.

The Friendship Level

Playing together, working together, planning together, laughing together, and crying together are ways of developing and maintaining friendship in a marriage.

During acute grief these joint activities lose their meaning. They may be downright painful. The joy and laughter are gone. The emotional tone of the relationship is flat.

If the husband and wife acknowledge that the joy is gone and that this is normal, their expectations of each other will be more realistic.

Spontaneous sharing of friendship may come to a halt during grief. As long as the couple can say, "This won't last," the marriage won't suffer.

One couple I know felt miles apart for the first ten months of grief. Smiles and light spirited moments were scarce. Then one day the two of them were doing dishes. The husband came up behind his wife and tickled her. She jumped away from him. He pursued. They ended up embracing and laughing on the couch. The joys of friendship had survived the dark times.

The Emotional Level

In friendship you discover the emotional needs of your spouse. When the emotional needs of both husband and wife are met, the marriage is fulfilling.

In grief the friendship suffers. Emotional needs are not met. Most people who are in acute grief are very dependent on others. Emotions are in a state of upheaval. Meeting ones own emotional needs is paramount. The marriage partner is bound to feel neglected.

Apart from grief it's unreasonable to expect your spouse to meet all your emotional needs. Why should you expect your spouse to meet all your needs during grief?

Close friends, pastors, counselors, and support groups are excellent resources during the early period of grief. Help shouldn't be sought secretly. Your spouse needs to know why you are seeking help and be aware of your resource. Obtaining support early is the key to maintaining equilibrium in the marriage.

The Communication Level

Marriage counselors place a lot of emphasis on the place of good communication in a marriage. This level must be fine-tuned regularly to keep a marriage strong.

Grief erodes this level. The temptation to keep things to yourself in order to prevent your spouse's further hurt is very strong. Talking may cause that sharp pain in your chest, bring tears and a nasty headache. Silence seems the better part of wisdom.

Sometimes the expression of feelings is met by a judgmental attitude or a sermon. This stifles the expression of feelings and closes down communication.

I suggest that a couple agree on a few simple rules of communication.

Rule # 1 - Check with your spouse to see if he or she is up to listening and sharing. If not, agree on a time that is convenient in the very near future.

Rule # 2 - Try not to do a lot of talking when it's late or when either of you is tired.

Rule # 3 - Allow your spouse to express whatever he or she feels without analyzing the feelings.

Rule # 4 - Touch each other tenderly while you talk. Feel free to hold each other when sadness overcomes one or both of you.

Rule # 5 - If your spouse doesn't have much to say, accept his or her silence.

Rule # 6 - If your spouse expresses anger, don't personalize it.

The Social Level

There are many reasons why marriage requires a social level. Relationships with others are a healthy way of meeting some of the needs your spouse cannot meet. Reaching out to others keeps the marriage from becoming self-centered. The influence of the home was designed by God to leaven society in a positive way.

Grief is a time when people often withdraw from others. People who once socialized with you tend to stay away. They stay away because they don't know what to say, because they think they might be intruding or because they have not dealt with their own losses. These and other reasons keep people away at a time when your need for support is enormous.

Grieving couples don't feel like socializing as much as they did because they are physically and emotionally exhausted. Spontaneous waves of sorrow and tears wash over them unannounced. This could be highly embarrassing in a social situation.

Reduction of social life means that husband and wife spend more time at home. Nerves already on edge become more edgy. Arguments and irritability are at an all-time high. The marriage is bound to suffer.

I suggest that couples keep social life simple during grief. Keep the engagements short and few, especially during the first year. Accept invitations from people you know best and with whom you feel the most comfortable. Agree before you go out that either spouse can shorten the visit. Make sure that both of you feel good about the engagement from the beginning.

The Physical Level

This is the level of marriage that provides shelter, clothes, food and little extras of comfort for mutual well-being.

Grief sometimes changes the physical environment. The wife may become careless about personal hygiene. Her hair may not be as well cared for as usual. The house may be untidy. She may not feel up to fixing her usual tasty meals.

The husband may not shave on his days off. The yard may go unmowed. Repairs around the house may be neglected. The usual precision in the workshop may have gone by the wayside.

The energy levels are low. Motivation is down. Maybe both spouses simply don't care. Nothing around the house has meaning. The attitude may be one of - "Why bother?"

I suggest that the grieving couple relax. Expecting too much of each other at this time is unreasonable. If it doesn't get done right away, don't worry. Tell yourself that you won't always feel this way.

It's more important to share feelings and get extra physical rest than to keep an immaculately clean house.

Getting upset about the lawn or the laundry will drive a wedge between two people when they need to be closer than ever before.

Good-hearted neighbors and a caring church can really help a grieving couple by doing some of the physical duties around the house.

The Sexual Level

If you picture the levels of marriage as a building, you will understand why the sexual level is disturbed during grief. When the foundations of a building crack and shift, cracks appear in the rest of the house. When grief cracks the lower levels of the marriage relationship you are bound to see and feel the effects in the upper levels. The sexual level is at the very top of the marriage relationship. This level is affected by the tremors set off by the shattering experience of loss.

Sexual intercourse during grief is comforting for some people. Some have mentioned that it helps them to feel real and alive. Others feel that this is a way to give their spouse a little pleasure at a time when pleasure is almost impossible to come by.

For some people the sex drive almost dies during acute grief. They see intercourse as an insult to the person who died. They can see no reason for having sexual pleasure when a loved one has been deprived of life. Some people report that they simply tolerate intercourse for the sake of their spouse.

During grief you need to remember that sexuality is more than intercourse. Thoughtful and unexpected kindnesses shown to your spouse arouse strong feelings of appreciation. Frequent use of the words - I love you - create a much needed sense of wholeness. When your spouse is crying, warm and tender embraces draw the two of you into oneness. Spontaneous hugs and kisses during the course of daily activities can lighten the heavy load of grief. Going for a walk hand-in-hand speaks eloquently of your deep affection.

If your spouse has trouble with this level, be just as patient as you were about the other levels. Your patience will create a richer quality to this level and to all the other levels of your marriage.

The myth that loss brings a husband and wife closer needs to be dispelled. Loss is a strain on every marriage relationship. If the marriage was weak before the loss, it may be in grave danger after the loss. A strong marriage isn't free from perils. Be alert to the little cracks in your marriage equilibrium. Feel free to seek professional help.

I have concluded that healing after the loss of a child is never complete. There will always be an element of relationship missing in the heart of the parent. When you are seated across the dining room table from your spouse, you are looking into the eyes of a person who has been wounded. His or her life is still tinged with sorrow.

Continued sensitivity and gentleness toward your spouse will have an ongoing healing effect. Going to special places together and springing pleasant surprises draws you close. Expressing appreciation and approval nullifies feelings of worthlessness that often come after a loss.

After the acute pain has subsided you need to build a store of pleasant memories. Take a long trip you always wanted to take. Plan some activities that are romantic. Take time to play together. In time you and your spouse will be able to look back on memories other than those associated with loss.

We are all molded by the events of daily life. This means that in subtle ways we are different every day. Your spouse is a different person every morning he or she wakes up in the bed next to you. This is particularly true when you lose a child. The two of you will never be the same again. Adjustments to these changes take time. If they are made within the framework of affection and understanding, your marriage will become a greater blessing to you. There will be rough places, but you will surmount them and climb to loftier heights of oneness.

Helpful Exercises

1. If you are married, ask your spouse to spend a quiet time with you to talk about your personal needs. Share how you think he or she can meet those needs. Do the same for your spouse. Refer to the levels of a relationship listed in this chapter.

2. Make a list of the things you'd like to do to encourage your spouse during a time of loss.

3. If you know a married couple who successfully adjusted to a loss, ask them to share ideas that worked for them.

12

Grief and the Family

I have followed many families from the emergency room through the long months of grief. No two families have been alike. Differences in culture, family customs, religious traditions and personality types figured into the varied reactions to loss. From my association with families in grief, I have concluded that the key to family recovery is allowing for individual differences.

The fabric of family unity weakens and crumbles when all family members are expected to grieve in the same way or at the same pace.

Many people face compound losses, but those losses are overlooked in the presence of the immediate family loss. Unresolved personal losses complicate adjustment to the present loss. When these complications go unrecognized, a smoldering process begins that ultimately reduces family solidarity to ashes.

A good example of this is the woman whose father died. She was hysterical at the hospital. Her brothers and sisters were critical of her reactions because they knew she wasn't close to her father. Their attitude caused her to cut off her contacts with the family.

This woman suffered a miscarriage six months before her father died. Her mother, with whom she was very close, died three years earlier, but she never allowed herself to believe it. Her siblings weren't aware of these complications.

Family members should understand that there is usually a high risk person in every family. Hysterical behavior, little or no display of emotion, unusually strong dependence on the person who has died, strong expression of anger and bitterness, strong feelings of self-reproach, a history of difficulty in adjusting to loss, and a history of emotional problems are clues that the person needs help, not criticism.

High risk people may go into a deep depression if adequate support is not readily available. Early support and long-term care is mandatory.

A grieving person should never feel cut off from his or her family. Some general understandings within the family will facilitate adjustment and prevent this cutting off process.

1. If you need time and space to be alone and quiet, let the family know. You'll be given your time and space.

2. If you need closeness, touching or a listening ear, let the family know. You'll receive intimacy.
3. You don't need to hide your sorrow or cry alone. When tears burn their way down your cheeks, you can cry with a family member.
4. We will get the family together periodically to assess how each person is adjusting. We won't take recovery for granted.
5. Holidays and anniversaries during the first year of grief will be times to talk about the missing person. Some sorrow will be expected, but we'll also plan to do something together as a family.
6. Flare-ups and short tempers may be caused by the gradual buildup of unexpressed sorrow. We'll try not to take it personally.
7. You may adjust to the loss sooner than others in the family. Be patient. Everybody grieves at a different pace.
8. If your family isn't meeting your needs, feel free to seek help outside of your family circle. Family members each have high levels of grief. This make it difficult to meet the needs of others.
9. Remember that other family members probably hurt as much as, or more than, you do. Treat them with tenderness.
10. Understand that the world soon forgets about your loss. Outside support is withdrawn too soon. Don't let this make you bitter. Spend your energy drawing together as a family.

Children in a family are often overlooked during great loss. "They're too little to understand" is a common statement. They may be too little to understand all the implications of loss, but they aren't too little to have feelings.

John Bowlby, a psychiatrist from England, has done extensive study in the area of children and loss. He believes that much research remains to be done, but he sticks to his view that children from six months to adolescence respond to loss in much the same way that adults respond to loss. Children may have increased sensitivity to the conditions that precede, surround and follow a major loss.

Chronological age and emotional maturity influence how children react and adjust to loss, but the child's environment is even more influential.

What the child is told is important. This was demonstrated to me at a funeral. A little boy asked why his "granny" died. A man standing nearby said, "Sonny, your granny died because God needed another angel." The little boy was disturbed to think that

God would take his one and only "granny" when heaven was already full of angels.

How the child is told sets the tone for the child's grief. If lots of euphemisms are used, the child may fantasize longer. If terms like "sleep" or "gone away" are used, the child may fear going to bed or interpret a person's "going away" as death.

When the child is told can prolong grief needlessly. A decision not to tell the child is often overridden by sad expressions on the faces of other family members. I've heard of children who aren't told about the death of a grandparent for months. By the time they know, the rest of the family have made a fairly complete recovery. The child is then left to grieve alone.

Children grieve well when their relationships with the missing person were rewarding. When the relationships were poor, the child may blame himself or herself for the death.

Adults in the child's environment affect the child's level of adjustment. If adults in the family don't talk about the death, never show emotion, or are insensitive to the reactions of the child, progress toward adjustment for the child may be impeded.

Children need plenty of touching, stroking, holding and constant reassurance that their needs will be met. If the child has lost a parent, steady care must be given by a few people. Being taken from one place to another for care could postpone the child's grief.

The child who doesn't have intimate relationships during early grief may adopt coping behaviors that are detrimental. Such a child may find it difficult to adjust to subsequent losses throughout life.

I'm very concerned about the weakening of family solidarity in America. I fear that many children who lose today may be in deep trouble tomorrow simply because of the reduced support from family. Adults come to my office for pastoral care because they're still angry about rejection and abandonment that occurred during their childhood.

I taught school for 5 years, pastored churches for 20 years, and served as a hospital chaplain for 13 years. During that time I met children who hurt inside, but they could no longer cry. I've seen them withdraw, run away from home, develop phobias, overeat, refuse nourishment, become hyperactive, and skip school. I've observed them breaking things apart because that's the way they felt deep inside - broken. These patterns are common among children who have lost family closeness.

A grandmother came to my office for help after her husband died. She always brought her 4-year-old grandson with her. While grandmother talked, little Jeb hyperactively explored my closets. He climbed on and over the chairs. He raced his toy car at high speeds over my rug.

One day I took Jeb on my lap. I asked him if he'd like to tell me about his grandfather. He readily related that he and grandfather went fishing together, ate breakfast together at 'Randy's Place, played ball together, and went riding in the van. He told about the sickness and the death. Jeb told me he cried when his grandfather was sick. He had a few tears running down his cheeks as he told me about his grandfather being "put under the ground."

I hugged Jeb close to me for a few minutes before he slid off my lap. He lay on the floor pushing his toy car. The car went slower and slower until Jeb was sound asleep.

During each of the following visits Jeb and I had our little chat together. Each time Jeb curled up on the soft rug next to my chair and took a nap.

Jeb settled it for me. Children need as much attention as grownups when it comes to grieving.

Adolescents are on an express train to independence, and I don't mean Independence, Missouri. This trip toward independence makes it difficult for them to lean on others during grief. They may deny having sad feelings and remain aloof from family.

I've worked with adolescents whose behavior is troubling to adults. Scrapes with the law, runaway episodes, drug abuse, alcohol abuse and truancy are just a few of their grief-related behaviors.

A classic example is the 16-year-old boy picked up three times for shoplifting. He pounded his fists on my desk and wept out, "I want my mom back. I want my mom back."

Sometimes adolescents confide in peers, but more than likely they keep their feelings to themselves. Those troubled feelings often show up later in antisocial decorum.

Support for adolescents needs to be gentle, low-key and nonconfrontive. The helper needs to be patient, friendly, genuine and willing to share himself or herself with the grieving adolescent.

When I relate to grieving teens I try to get several ideas across to them. First, you're bound to have some strong and painful feelings. Second, these feelings are normal. Third, having these feelings doesn't mean that you aren't mature. Fourth, I have the same feelings when I lose. Fifth, you'll adjust better if you share your feelings with another person. Sixth, I'll be glad to listen, but I won't be upset if you find someone else easier to talk to. This approach doesn't threaten their independence.

Jack and Andy lost their mother in a tragic accident. When they came to see me four months later they talked about hockey and basketball. They were on the school's teams. I patiently joined in their humorous conversation. After two sessions they knew they could trust me not to push my way into their feelings. They finally accepted my initial offer to share their pain.

The reward for patience came when Jack spoke up for the both of them. "We sure thank you for helping us. We didn't know what was happening to us. Now we understand. We can make it from here. If we get in a jam we'll be sure to get back to see you."

Death and dying classes for junior high school students can be beneficial. When students understand the dynamics of grief, they're less apt to avoid fellow students who are grieving. Peer support can be very therapeutic to the adolescent.

Older family members are frequently overlooked when there is a major loss in the family. They feel neglected and abandoned.

If small children need cuddling and assurances of continuing care, so do elderly family members. Why is it that we fondle and coo over the newborn, but seldom touch the people who are coming to the close of life? When elderly people are grieving they need intimacy with their loved ones. They need to talk about their feelings and reminisce with the rest of the family.

There's a song that says, "Folks don't kiss old people any more." Kissing, talking to and hugging the elderly is still in style. I hope the words to that song are incorrect.

Honesty and openness are the two qualities needed when a family grieves. Patience is the third quality that is indispensable when a family member does not choose to face the reality of loss right away.

Some children refuse to talk about a dead parent. The remaining parent longs to share feelings with the child, but the child refuses. This refusal may last for years. The parent's best option is to say, "I'll never push you to talk. I just want you to know that I'll be here to listen and share when you're ready."

If the child is ready after the parent has made many adjustments to the loss of a spouse, the parent may have to preface the conversation in this way. "I want you to know that I've made many adjustments to our loss. If I share without lots of tears, it's not because I'm calloused or indifferent. Please don't be angry with me if my feelings are not as intense as yours. They were at one time, but, thank God, I've experienced some healing."

As you can see, dealing with a belated griever requires much patience and tact.

With continuing honesty, openness and patience, the chances of a family growing together through loss are great. A family will never be the same after a loss, but hopefully, the positive aspects of recovery will far outweigh the negative side effects.

Families mistakenly assign roles to individuals to fill the place of the missing person. I met a man and a woman who had been sweethearts for 40 years, but they didn't marry because of assigned roles. The man's widowed mother extracted a promise from him that he would not marry until she died. His mother gave him the role of caregiver. The woman's widowed mother gave the same role. Both mothers died about the same time. Finally the couple married in their sixth decade of life.

"You have to be the big sister now." "You'll be the daddy from now on. You'll have to see that the lawn is mowed and that the wood supply is gathered for winter." "I'll have to depend on you to get the meals now that Mother is gone." These assignments can rob children of their childhood and cause resentment.

Sometimes people assume roles they are neither asked to take nor qualified to take. Families who have periodic family conferences should be on the lookout for these unfair role assumptions.

A friend in Ohio heard her 8-year-old son say, "I'm the man of the house now. I'll do Dad's work for him." She talked to her son. "Allen, I'm thankful that you want to help around the house. You're a good boy and I love you, but I can't allow you to be the father. I am the mother, you are the son, but there is no father now. But we are still a family. If I do my part by being a good mother and you continue to be a good son, we'll do real well as a family."

A family discontinued their usual socializing after a two-year-old baby died. Thanksgiving gatherings, Christmas parties, and birthday celebrations were cancelled. This was especially upsetting to one person in the family. She concocted all sorts of situations designed to force and even trick the family to get together. She actually built barriers instead of tearing them down. My advice was to leave the family alone. Don't maneuver and coerce. In time someone will initiate the renewal of family togetherness. A year after the death a daughter invited her parents for dinner. After that the family slowly renewed traditional family get-togethers.

When I first began bereavement support groups, I advised people to go outside of the family for support. My reason was that all family members were so engulfed by the pain of grief that none of the members were able to get past their own grief. But after observing many families in grief, I have changed my views.

I now believe the family is the best support system available during grief. Families have learned to love, fight, reconcile, resolve conflict, and face crises. When the world has forgotten, the family still remembers. Sharing memories with a family member is much more therapeutic than reminiscing with a person who scarcely knew the missing person. The family may have ups and downs, fight like cats and dogs, and hold grudges, but they know how to lift your load when it becomes too heavy.

Helpful Exercises

1. Sit down with members of your family. Look through photograph albums and memento collections. Share stories of the family history. Allow photographs of the missing person to be the basis for reviewing memories.

2. Think about each member of your family. Whom do you think may have the most difficulty adjusting to loss? Visit with him or her. Agree on ways to make adjustment easier.

3. Review how previous losses have shattered your family. How have they drawn the family together?

13

Intentional Grieving

Much of the grief I have observed during the last 22 years has been haphazard. People have been swept along by a flood of emotions, but like victims of a raging flash flood, they have had no choice in the matter. The emotions came over them instantly and furiously. When the initial fury briefly subsided, they tried to avoid further contact with the reminders of their loss. They hoped they could somehow escape any further contact with reality.

Edward is a case in point. He lost two children in the same disaster. Helplessly he went to work. Painfully he drove home in tears. He didn't know what to do to ease the pain, so he remained the victim of his grief that struck him with wavelike unpredictability. He was afraid to look at pictures of the children. Going into their bedroom was impossible.

"There must be something I can do to prevent grief from rendering me helpless at the most awkward times and places, but I don't know what it is," he said.

I shared with him an approach to grieving that occurred to me ten years ago. I have shared it with many people who found it extremely helpful. Let me share it with you.

Reserve a time slot for grieving each day. Pick a time when you will be undisturbed. Choose a place where you will feel free to talk aloud to yourself and cry. The length of this quiet time is up to you. Just make sure that you spend the time daily. Tell yourself that it is time for you to grieve. This takes away some of the haphazardness. You will begin to have a sense of control.

Provide some simple tools for your time of intentional grieving. You'll need a pencil, a notebook or journal, facial tissues, and a variety of objects that prompt memories such as portraits, snapshots, trinkets, articles of clothing, jewelry, and letters. These items will change from time to time to correspond with the part of the relationship you are reconstructing.

At the beginning of each session choose one part of the relationship that used to be but can be no longer. For example, you may have gone fishing together. Think about all the fishing trips you can recall. Look at snapshots of fishing trips. Handle favorite lures and rods. Write some of the highlights of those trips in your notebook. Describe the feelings you had about the time together. Briefly record the happy times and the not-so-happy times. Jot down comments that the person made. Discipline yourself to focus only on your fishing adventures. If your mind wanders, simply tell yourself that you'll think about that later. Then go back to your work of reconstructing and reliving your fishing trips.

This exercise forces you to review the life of the person. Frequently people in grief can think of nothing but the death. It is therapeutic to evaluate the worth of a person's life and the worth of your relationship with that person.

The exercise also requires you to experience some pain that you'd normally dismiss from your mind in seconds. In your quiet time of intentional grieving you face the pain longer. This allows the pain to lose its power to cut to the quick.

As you review one aspect of the relationship you will usually become aware that you will not experience it again in this life. This awareness is a crucial component of adjusting to your loss. Now is the time to confirm this reality.

In your notebook write a short farewell to doing what you can no longer do. Say your farewell directly and clearly.

Now that you have written the short farewell, read it aloud to yourself. Read it many times. You'll soon be able to say it without reading. Say it from your heart. The tears may come and the sobs may interrupt the flow of words. Don't attempt to stop the tears. Let them flow as you repeat the farewell. Keep repeating it until the sobbing subsides.

Your whole body will feel tense after many of your sessions. Lie on the floor face up. Tell yourself that your body is heavy and sinking through the floor. Breathe deeply and slowly. Remain in this relaxed position for at least ten minutes. Rise from the floor and end your time of intentional grieving by saying a simple prayer of thanks for the time you shared with that special person. You may want to create your own way of concluding each session.

Intentional grieving times focus the emotions that might otherwise become vague or blurred. When the emotions are tied to one aspect of the relationship, you are more likely to notice movement in your adjustment to your loss. Movement is the goal, not time. Don't concern yourself with how long grief lasts. Watch for movement toward adjustment. Intentional grieving sessions can prevent getting stuck in some part of the grieving process.

I have noticed that men appreciate this approach because men like to fix things and take charge. This organized method gives them some control, something they can do about grief. They can see progress even though it be in small increments.

Even though an increasing number of men have been attending bereavement support groups, many men still believe they can grieve on their own. Quiet and regular sessions in the privacy of the home, following a simple procedure, give men a constructive alternative to attending a group or keeping busy to forget.

Ideally a grieving person should have at least one support person with whom he or she can talk. Keeping a notebook or journal during intentional grieving sessions provides a good source of discussion when sharing with a support person. I encourage people to bring their written material to their sessions with me. It is especially helpful to read farewells to another person.

Your written material is an excellent resource for helping you determine whether you are moving toward adjustment. This is done by periodically reading your journal from the beginning. If your reading triggers less pain, you will know that you have made progress. The general content will also reveal movement.

A nurse gave me permission to use her journal to illustrate how intentional grieving promotes movement toward adjustment.

Five weeks after her husband died she wrote, "I'm beginning to know you're really gone. No, I don't really believe you're gone yet. Not yet!"

Two months after her loss she wrote, "I feel such loneliness and sadness, but the terrible anguish I felt the first weeks is slowly easing up. I try now to think of ways to live without you. I pray for strength to go on."

Three months after the death she wrote, "I think today was the turning point. I think I'm beginning to accept your death. It's final. Tonight I'm calm. No tears tonight. I miss you. I wish you were beside me to kiss me goodnight. Never again though will you do that, nor will I be able to touch you or say I love you except to your picture or your memory."

At the end of the fifth month she wrote, "Tomorrow is our anniversary- 34 years. I've had a good day. Don't know if it's because I've been so busy or if God's answered my prayer for peace."

After six months she wrote, "I think I've entered a new phase of this grief. It's reality now. You're gone forever and I'm alive. I want to be alive. I want to enjoy living again."

These few excerpts from her journal reveal a movement toward life without her husband. As I reviewed the journal with her, she marveled at the progress she had made in six months. Much of that was due to her willingness to grieve intentionally.

14

Be Good to Yourself

When great losses come to us we sometimes feel that there is no use going on. Our self-esteem is greatly diminished. We see no reason to take care of ourselves because we are worthless - or so we think.

I frequently meet people in grief who have become so convinced of their worthlessness that they eat poorly, dress in poor taste, and practice grooming habits far inferior to their usual standards. Almost total immobilization sets in. Rarely do they go out of the house. Newspapers, books and magazines of interest go untouched.

If this is happening to you, make a careful study of the fifteenth chapter of the Gospel According to Luke. The key lesson of the three stories in that chapter is that God places an enormous amount of value on each person, even when we are very disappointed with our own failures. We may feel worthless and rejected, but our value in God's sight has not changed. This is very important for a grieving person to understand.

Move another step toward the realization that your potential for loving others and living creatively still exists. The object of your love may be gone so that there is no love given in response to yours, but your potential for loving is the same. Love is of God. The source of love has not dried up. Your potential for living creatively is unchanged. The person who shared in much of your creativity is gone, but creativity only waits to be shared with others.

You still have life. Life is a gift that cannot tolerate being kept in a box. It must be shared for the benefit of others if it's to thrive.

If you decide to withdraw from others and live in the past for the rest of your life, you are only hurting yourself more than you already hurt. Healing comes by reaching out and using the beautiful commodity - your God-given life.

Be good to yourself and move out into life. Not too fast at first, you understand. Move out a step at a time. It's possible to move out of the circle of grief prematurely. One way of knowing if you're doing this is when every little action requires force on your part and you're extremely exhausted.

Some women take little steps like making a pie "from scratch" instead of taking one from the freezer, or writing a letter to a person who needs to be encouraged. Some men go to the hardware store for supplies and then fix a leaky faucet, or they may wash and wax the car.

Be good to yourself by getting a good physical examination. When the doctor gives you his assessment, ask him what kind of exercise would be suitable for you. Keep the exercise program interesting and within your physical limits, but, whatever you do, keep active.

Grief has a way of tightening up the muscles of your body so that you don't breathe deeply. This tightening can be eliminated by proper exercise. Perhaps a vigorous walk concluded by a leisurely stroll of equal length would be ideal for most people.

Death or divorce are the greatest stressors to the human system. They bring changes that require many adjustments. To add more change on top of one of these major changes is asking for real trouble. As much as possible, avoid changes for the first year or so. Your adjustment to a major loss will be much easier if you can keep all of the other areas of life stable.

Friends and family may advise you to sell the house, change jobs, move away, or have somebody come and live with you, but this is not the best advice in most cases. If circumstances are such that these changes are necessary, fine. In most cases it is wise to wait until you have been able to resolve the grief.

Stress is unavoidable. The days following the loss will bring their conflict. Learning how to handle conflict is important. Let me share a few ideas.

1. When conflict arises don't act on a whim. Slow down. Pray to God for wisdom and perspective.
2. Talk with a friend who can help you discover the origin of your conflict.
3. Think it through very carefully. This can be done by listing all the possible options and the possible results of following each of these options.
4. Choose one or two options that you feel are the best and do what you can about them. Be careful to do what can be done today, today, and put off what can't be done until tomorrow for tomorrow, and forget about that which is out of your control.

These four tips help when the crisis comes, but improving your coping skills is a long-range project. I like to call our coping ability our cool range. It is something like a temperature gauge on a car. Below a certain point is freeze-up. Above a certain point is boil-over.

This cool range can be narrowed by our lifestyle. Grief is the greatest pressure that narrows the cool range. When we experience grief we must be on guard against a host of other conditions that further narrow the range. Among these are fear, anger, discouragement, jealousy, envy, resentment, sedentary lifestyle, violence, excessive change, domestic strife, pressure to achieve, boredom, smoking, drugs, breakfast skipping, poor nutrition, underrest, overwork and alcohol.

On the positive side there are simple, yet effective measures we can take to broaden our cool range. Among these are the expression of gratitude to God and to mankind; the expression of affection, joy, forgiveness, courage, hope, peace and trust in God; an exercise program that suits our health; a good relaxation program; and good health habits.

As we're going through grief the pressures of life still keep coming at us. In fact, business matters related to settling estates or negotiating with insurance companies increase the things that cry for our attention. One woman told me, "I never knew my husband had business dealings with half of the people who are pushing for settlement."

It's helpful to think of our minds as filters. We decide which of the items coming at us will be labeled "discard," "unimportant," "can wait," "vital," or "top priority." Only a few items filter through as necessary in a given day.

I'm actually advocating that people in grief must be good to themselves by simplifying life each day. If someone has to wait a few more days or weeks because of your grief - so what? Grief is no picnic. You deserve a little pampering.

Shortly after our son died, friends took us to a Pennsylvania Dutch smorgasbord. They had also lost a child and probably sensed that we needed a special treat. We would not have done it on our own because we were numbed by our grief. Fourteen years later we stopped at the same restaurant. I reflected on how beneficial it was to have a change of scenery.

My personal way of being good to myself is to plan time for creative solitude. I tied my canoe to my car and headed for a dam 50 miles from home. I took a lunch and a thermos of hot chocolate. I paddled to the dam breast and pointed the canoe toward the opposite end. The wind was at my back so I lay down in the canoe and propped up my head on a cushion. As the wind pushed my craft I slept. At the end of the dam I was awakened by the waves lapping against the canoe and the noisy red-winged blackbirds protecting their nests. I ate lunch and then paddled upwind to my car. Because it was late October there wasn't another person at the dam. It was my world and my time for stretching my spiritual muscles.

I visited a woman who had lost her husband a year earlier. She had closed up her house and refused to answer her phone. In her reclusive state she had become depressed and physically frail. I immediately made my way to her front parlor. Through the large picture window I gazed at the large lake dotted with sailboats. The stimulating resort town lay before her, but she was a prisoner because she had chosen to suffer. For an hour I challenged her to be good to herself. I told her that there is a time to grieve, but there must also be a time to let people, places and things draw us away from our pain.

A widow in Texas found a fascinating way to be good to herself. On Thanksgiving and Christmas she served dinner to hundreds of people. A philanthropist financed the meals in the large city of Fort Worth, Texas. Some of the guests were homeless, some were friendless and some were sickly, but all were welcomed into the warmth of a large banquet hall. The Texas widow brought them food, hugged them, laughed with them and sang with them. Without realizing it, she had done herself a greater favor.

Yes, I know you don't feel like doing yourself a favor, but do it anyway. You deserve it. You are special.

Helpful Exercise

1. Make a list of experiences that you think would help you to feel relaxed and worthwhile. Schedule those experiences and begin benefitting from them.

15

CPR

During a grief recovery seminar I was making the point that readjustment to life after the loss of a loved one must begin in three areas - relationship, communication and participation. A young woman spoke up and said, "Larry, if you rearrange those terms you'd have CPR."

The idea intrigued me. I rearranged them immediately - communication, participation and relationship.

Death, divorce and other types of major losses are a threat to emotional, physical, social and spiritual well-being. Life comes to a standstill for many grieving people. They despair of ever getting over their loss. Frequently they say to me, "I feel dead inside," "I will never be interested in living again," or "I feel like a part of me has died."

There is a serious need to "resuscitate," if you please, the people suffering from the loss of significant personal relationships. I will share the CPR process with you.

Communication

When a person loses a loved one, communication takes a major blow. Love and trust enabled them to talk about everything. There was a transparency between them that permitted them to share common chatter of the day as well as personal intimacies. They could test new ideas and challenge old ideas without losing their standing with each other. They could express affection and be sure of a positive response. But death changes all of this. Communication, in its ideal state, is vanished.

At first the survivor is compelled to talk about the one who died. Hours will be spent reviewing the events surrounding the death. Friends who call at the funeral home will each hear an array of memories of the person who died. It is an urge to communicate about the person. This urge to communicate about is not always carried out in actual practice. Unfortunately, some people find it difficult to talk. They fear the emotional pain of expression.

Grieving people sometimes become silent. They do not talk to their close family members, let alone their casual friends. Communication may deteriorate to the point of complete isolation. Yet, inside, the urge to express feeling is raging.

Scores of people in my seminars tell me that they never have been able to talk about feelings. Some tell about deaths that occurred much earlier in life for which there was almost no emotional release through talking.

One person remarked, "I just can't bring myself to talk about it. Come to think of it, I came from a family that kept things to themselves."

A friend of mine went four years before she talked to anyone about her son's death during the war in Vietnam.

In some cases people long to talk about the death of a loved one for months and months after the funeral, but those who listened at the time of the funeral are no longer in the mood to listen.

At other times the grieving person feels that talking to friends about the loss is an imposition. They withdraw for fear of driving people away. In actuality, the friends may welcome the chance to support and their unwillingness may only be imagined by the hurting person.

Within families the lines of communication sometimes deteriorate. There develops an unspoken agreement that nobody will bring up the topic. If one member mentions the dead person, he or she will get the response, "I don't want to hear about it."

The environment of our society doesn't make it easy to talk about sad feelings. At times a grieving person feels that there is no place to talk about them. Nobody seems to care enough to listen. Their analysis is not always wrong.

It may be necessary for a grieving person to seek out people in the helping professions such as a pastor, family counselor or physician.

Mutual support groups and group seminars provide the opportunity to reestablish communication again.

Those who venture into new and renewed avenues of verbalization seem to gain a measure of control over circumstances that seem beyond control. The pain, that was at first almost unbearable, grows less acute.

After five weeks of grief therapy I frequently hear people say, "It's so much easier to talk about it now than it was five weeks ago. When I first came to this group I could barely introduce myself without getting all choked up."

A very dear friend of mine attended Grief Recovery just two weeks after his wife died in his arms. He was unable to say "good evening" without sobbing between words. People in the group were patient with him. They encouraged him to talk in spite of the tears. In a few weeks he was talking about his wife with only an occasional catch in his voice. The pain subsided as he expressed himself and reopened the lines of communication with those around him.

So much of what we do in life involves people we love. When

those people die, the activities become meaningless and downright depressing.

So much attention is given to the loss itself that there is no psychic energy left to do anything else.

Participation

Participation in the usual activities of life is the ultimate step toward recovery. Engaging the total personality in constructive action is the ideal, but it can only happen by starting slowly. You gradually expand your participation until you have experienced a new feeling of adequacy for the tasks of life.

Overwhelming feelings of guilt sometimes nag at people when they first get involved again. Going to a party and engaging in laughter creates feelings of disloyalty to their dead loved one. The first real urge to socialize with a person of the opposite sex causes a widow or widower to feel guilty. Going on a family picnic after the death of a child produces all kinds of mixed emotions. This is to be expected. Don't let it deter you from reinvolvement.

Returning to work and church presents some anxiety. Fear of "breaking down" is uppermost in some people's minds.

As a rule, if people permit themselves to verbalize feelings freely and to weep openly in the privacy of their home, the need to cry in public is not as great. Some people go back to work part-time for a few weeks before resuming the full-time responsibility. I encourage people to go back to church a step at a time. One week arrive late and leave early. If you can't take the hymns, just come for the sermon. As time goes by you'll be able to enjoy the whole church service.

A saying I use in group therapy goes like this: "It is easier to act your way into a new way of feeling than it is to feel your way into a new way of acting."

It is true, if you wait until you feel like going to your club meetings, you may not do it for years. If you determine to go - feel like it or not - you will get back into the swing of it again. You will eventually look forward to the chance to be with your friends.

Ideally you would do well to participate in activities that you enjoy. Eliminate the things you once did for the sake of togetherness, but that you didn't particularly like. Your lifestyle can now be altered to suit your needs.

Relationship

In an earlier chapter, I mentioned the uprootedness of American society that has diminished the circle of supporting intimate relationships. This makes grief more difficult. This condition can be corrected by what I call "reaching out."

Much of the intense grief work involves receiving on the part of the person in grief. Once the acute stages of grief are past, it is time to start giving as well as receiving.

Frequently when I counsel with clients who suffer from a lack of relationships, I tell them to make their way to the nearest convalescent home.

"Go to the administrator's office and ask if there is one lonely person who needs a visit," I advise, "And when you visit, do twice as much listening as you do talking. Let that old-timer tell you about the good old days. Before you leave, tell that person how grateful you are. Let him or her know that your life is much richer for the sharing."

Americans, in general, have been suffering from the reduction of dialogue in meaningful relationships. There is less reaching out and more "every man for himself" in our age of technology. But changing the picture lies within each person.

Have you ever ridden on an elevator and noticed how nobody speaks? They just look up at the floor numbers and watch them light up one-by-one. Try reaching out the next time you ride an elevator. It can be exciting. Yes, I know you may never see those people again, but their responses to your reaching out can be a means of making you whole again.

What about the relationships that you already have? Have they become stale? Perhaps they can be revived. One way of doing that is by having your friends over for a meal. Take an interest in them. Ask questions about their hobbies or latest trip. Be open with them. Tell them what your relationship means to you. Express gratitude for their friendship.

Write letters to the relatives who live out of town. Bring them up to date and inquire about their health. Share pictures and send unexpected tokens of your friendship.

My wife had an "auntie" in Washington, D.C., who was widowed for many years, but she experienced more relatedness than most people you meet. If the PTA needed someone to do a funny or sad reading, "Auntie" was the first person they thought of. She wrote her own. At Christmas time the card from "Auntie" was the most welcome - home made and personalized. When our children were little and spilling things, "Auntie" had us over for a meal. The apartment was small, but tray tables did the trick. She couldn't have cared less about a spill. "Auntie" was still making new friends when a lot of people were running out of them. Her secret was reaching out.

Many health professionals who are concerned about caring for the whole person are talking about relationship from another angle.

Love, relatedness, purpose and meaning in life have their source in a relationship with God. Illness and major crises such as death, divorce and rejection have a way of impairing a person's ability to be aware of God's desire for a relationship. This causes a person to feel hopeless, unloved and unforgiven.

What it amounts to is a temporoary loss of faith. This may make it difficult for a person to feel good about self and others.

Reestablishing relationships is hindered, then, unless there can be a reconciliation with the Source of relationships.

When the numbness of grief strikes, a person is often powerless to do this on his or her own. It frequently takes another person, serving as a catalyst, to bring about the CPR of recovery and the renewal of faith.

The following acrostic will describe what is involved in being that catalyst that facilitates recovery. If you are grieving, don't be afraid to lean on this kind of a person. If you are recovered from grief, it will give you a goal to strive for in being helpful to others who sorrow.

C — Care given out of concern

A — Assessment of the total needs of the grieving person that enables one to better anticipate the needs of the sorrowing

T — Tact

A — Attention to the little extras that make a grieving person feel good about self

L — Listening love. This is listening at deeper levels of hurt and healing

Y — Your own relationship with God that in turn influences your attitude toward others

S — Skill in giving emotional support

T — Time to be with the grieving person

Once persons establish communication, participation and relationship they begin to see life with more perspective. They are able to concentrate not on what they have lost, but on what they have left.

CPR was required training for all hospital employees. The week after I received my certificate I visited an older woman on the medical ward. She had just gone into pulmonary arrest. I pulled the emergency cord and asked the operator to announce "Code Blue" for room 316. Then I began to administer CPR. In just a minute or two at the most, that room filled with people and crash carts. They relieved me and carried on the resuscitation with amazing skill and precision.

I've noticed that such a rapid response does not come for people in grief. They suffer emotional arrest, pull the cord and call "Code Blue," but help does not come quickly. Sometimes it boils down to giving CPR to yourself. Doing so can be less frustrating and more beneficial than waiting for others to do it.

16

Walls That Close In

A 30-year-old woman struggled to get the words out. Slowly she said, "You'll never know how I long for someone to touch me. Someone to hold me. Just anyone. I thought we had a good marriage. It seemed like it to me. Little did I know that just weeks after the honeymoon he was seeing another woman. We stayed together for six months - long enough for me to get pregnant. Now my daughter is five. Just the two of us. She is a doll, but when it is all said and done, I am alone. I can't cling to her for my emotional support. It isn't fair. Every night I long to be in someone's arms. The desire for someone to touch me and say 'I love you' overpowers me. I feel the four walls of that house closing in on me. In desperation I bury my face in a pillow and cry until I fall asleep. Somehow, somewhere, there must be an answer for me."

Several people in the group were moved to tears and to action when they heard her cry for help. They went over to her and embraced her and spoke quiet words of comfort.

These were words of loneliness - symbols of painful loss. Every person in the group felt an aching of heart that cried out, "Something must be done."

A distraught mother fumbled with the doily on the arm of the couch in an effort to tell me the story without weeping. "He was so young and full of life. His great love was riding his bicycle. His bicycle took him to his death. You see, he rode it out onto the ice. We don't know if he fell and the weight of the fall broke the ice or whether he just hit a weak place in the ice. He didn't have a chance.

"Now I go into his bedroom and sit for a long time. I try to remember his voice and see his face when he was excited about something. I wait, thinking that maybe he'll just walk into the room and say, "Hi Mom,' but he never does. I know I have the other children, and my husband has been real good, but this house is so empty. I feel so alone."

The loneliness of this mother still tugs at my heart.

Loneliness seems to be a pre-packaged ingredient of grief. I have yet to meet a person who hasn't experienced it. There are some who go so far as to say that loneliness is a part of being human apart from grief. Others feel that there are chapters of loneliness that fit into every maturational stage of life ranging from loneliness due to birth to loneliness due to the abandonment of the aged.

I have learned from grieving people that loneliness hits you the hardest months after the funeral or divorce. They taught me that during the first few months of grief people are too busy being angry, guilty or numb with shock and denial to be lonely. When they care for all the business related to the separation and express the hostility against the doctors or family - then comes the incomparable loneliness of grief.

It has become obvious to me that when people do not fight grief, but let it happen as a normal human reaction to a great loss, they have sufficient coping power to manage their loneliness. The sooner and more intensely grieving is done in the early months after the loss, the easier it becomes to handle the situation of being alone.

If grieving people have adequate support systems during early grief, they very likely will have developed new and renewed relationships that will soften the blow of being alone.

Loneliness results from the sudden removal of a person's source of satisfaction of human hungers. That satisfaction can only take place via intimate personal relationships.

Over and over the recovered participants of Grief Recovery insist that you have to make up your mind that loneliness will not rule your life. That may be "easier said than done," but a lot of people have done it. Let me share some of the secrets they have shared with me.

1. Do your grieving early and intensely.

You don't have to be strong for others. You are not obligated to get back to normal so that others are confortable around you. Grief is a sign that you are healing and growing as a person. Let it happen.

2. After a reasonable length of intense grief, say good-bye to the relationship that was lost.

It is a psychological amputation that is vital to your overall health. Some people keep a journal and say good-bye in the journal. Others say good-bye to things they did with the person while holding his or her picture in front of them. Saying good-bye is a healthy closure to the period of intense grief.

Some of the comments I hear reveal the value of this closure.

"Once I said good-bye to doing everything with Ned I had the best day since he died. It was like a heavy responsibility had been lifted off my shoulders."

"After I wrote my farewell to Jim, I told my kids that we had been living in the past. Now we were going to live for each other and do things to make our lives count. I cleaned the house that day and we all ate a good supper."

"I said good-bye. Along with the good-bye came a release from the anger I had toward God and I wanted to get to know Him."

3. Begin to concentrate on your own life.

Lay short-term and long-term goals for using your talents and for developing new ones. Gradually break habit patterns based upon "the two of us" and move from the world of "we" into the world of "I." Build your self-identity and do things that you like to do. If you and your children are survivors from the death of a spouse, plan some things for the new-sized family. Make a calendar of events.

4. Look at solitude as a friend.

This is time for self-confrontation. Who am I? What can I become? How do I view life - as a drudge, a right or a gift? What are my values? Do I like myself? What areas of my life can I improve? Am I a giver or a taker? These are a few of the self-confrontational questions that can turn your solitude into growth adventures.

5. Become knowledgeable about the world around you.

Broaden your interests and be well-read. This expands the inner-person. A variety of challenging activities will make you an interesting person and put you in touch with interesting people. This is a good way to combat loneliness that leads to despair.

6. Volunteer your time.

Some people may find volunteering an effective preventive measure against loneliness. It depends on the person and on the type of service for which you are volunteering.

7. Grief produces fatigue.

For this reason a person should get adequate rest, plan a balanced diet and do plenty of big muscle exercise. Instead of wearing "old grubbies" all the time, dress up real sharp. You'll feel good about yourself. A person who feels good about his or her appearance will find it easier to reach out to others.

Loneliness often becomes a way of life for those who live in the past. Reliving the experiences of yesteryear robs the energy that could be used to make each new day a new chapter. Take from the past the lessons of value and then go beyond the achievements of days gone by.

The regrets of the past cannot be changed. Nobody has a chance for a rerun. All we can do is learn from our mistakes and try to make the present count.

Bringing more simplicity into life is a necessity if we are going to concentrate on the little graces of life that create meaning. Meaning must enter life before lonelines can be dispelled.

I received a card from an Oscar Smith. He checked the box marked, "I desire to know more about the Scriptures." Thinking I was about to meet a young man with very little knowledge of the Bible, I rang the doorbell and waited eagerly.

I suddenly heard a voice behind me. "Yes, what can I do for you?"

I turned and saw an old man with a cane in his hand. I told him I was responding to his card. His eyes twinkled as he invited me to his upstairs apartment.

"I have a great deal to learn and such a short time to learn it in. I know of the work of your church only slightly, but I must know more. Teach me all you can. I am open for more understanding," he pleaded.

Who was Oscar? A 99-year-old minister in the Advent Christian Church. Educated by the great preacher, Dwight L. Moody, Oscar had been preaching since he was 17. His wife had died five years earlier. Loneliness came to be his guest, but Oscar couldn't take time to entertain it. It soon left.

His dining room table was covered with correspondence and research papers in the process of being written. Several times a week he was taken to dinners for senior citizens where he served as the chaplain. His one goal was to bring Christians of all faiths into unity.

I attended Oscar's 100th birthday celebration at a senior citizen center. With interest I listened to the 10-minute sermon he had been preparing for some time. It was a masterpiece - the reading of the text, statement of purpose, three points, summary and application. His timing was exactly 10 minutes. He didn't have a single note from which to speak.

A middle-aged minister sitting next to me leaned over and whispered, "That old man makes my preaching sound sick."

My response was, "The reason he can preach so well at 100 is because he never stopped living."

Oscar was hospitalized just before he had his 100th birthday. This was a great concern to him because he was scheduled to make a presentation of books to the library of his alma mater. Catheterization was no obstacle to Oscar. On the morning of the presentation he talked the physician into giving him a 10-hour pass. The proper attachments were supplied and off he went to his seminary. By supper he was back in his hospital bed.

Oscar and I were like brothers. He shared with me the secret of creatively living alone. First of all he suffered from the death of his wife, but he concluded that life is a gift from God. In his grief he thanked God for sharing the life of a woman with him.

While Oscar didn't invite his great loss, he looked at grief as an experience of growth. He sought ways of adjusting that would dynamically change him from within.

He decided very early that once he worked his way through his grief, he would not be captive to the feelings of grief the rest of his life. He believed that we feel the way we choose to feel.

Within months of his wife's death Oscar began to reach out and lift others. The willingness to learn and lift others drew me to the old man. He soothed my troubled heart. His ministry to my soul cemented our relationship, guaranteeing Oscar that he would never be hopelessly lonely.

Oscar taught me that grief is like a picture projected out of focus on a screen. The larger objects can be made out with much effort, but the tiny details are completely lost in the blur. Recovery is the turning of the lens that brings the picture back into focus. As the focus sharpens, all the little details stand out in a way that complements the larger objects. In the end we can look at the whole with new appreciation.

Walls close in on those who refuse to reach out and dialogue with others.

Helpful Exercises

1. Have walls closed in on you? What are those walls? Make a list of practical actions you will take to remove the walls.

2. Do you have family members or friends who have been closed in by walls? Lay plans for helping them to tear down the walls. This is an excellent way to remove your own walls.

17

Take It From Me

I'm deeply indebted to the beautiful people who have attended Grief Recovery seminars over the last decade and a half for the material in this chapter. They have shared some very painful experiences with me. They have put in writing some of the ideas that have helped them. With their permission, I anonymously share their thoughts with the readers of this book.

None of my friends profess to know all the answers. They don't claim that their techniques are ideal or that they will work for everyone. They simply believe that sharing with others who are in a similar situation can be encouraging and therapeutic.

In response to my question about how they handled the loneliness, I received some good answers.

"At first I ran. At home I was so lonely that I felt just half a person. The other half of my being was gone. I couldn't read, watch TV or sit still. I just wandered from room to room. My motivation was gone. I had always loved to sew, but I couldn't now. I set limitations for myself, but I couldn't keep them. I misplaced and lost things. I started a dozen projects and didn't finish them. I stayed with my uncle for seven months. By April I was so homesick that I ran again. This time to home.

"Never before has the earth seemed so beautiful, nor have the birds sung so sweet. I suddenly found myself enjoying small things, the beautiful sunrise, the wind in the trees, a rose in blossom, baby rabbits on the lawn, even the smell of the air and the taste of our good water. It still surprises me. I thought the world had shut down. I was healing and the sun was still shining.

"After this long year I'm just beginning to realize that I can do what I want to without consulting anyone. I can read all night, sew right through meal time or turn off the TV if I don't like the programs. I am still very lonely at times, but I can fill my time with things I like to do. I can be alone without being lonely. I've always had a great many interests. Now I can pursue them without being self-limiting."

I shared the above thoughts because the author paints a pretty accurate picture of moving from despairing loneliness to healing and purposeful living. I hope you noticed that it took time.

One person was very wise when she said, "I could not handle the loneliness. I had to ask for help."

This person learned the value of expression. "The loneliness and lost feelings come and go, and at the strangest and most unexpected times. For instance, when you're shopping in the grocery store and you come across an item that your deceased mate especially liked to eat. I've learned that you must let go and cry right there in the store. It may be a little embarrassing for a few moments, but you do feel better afterwards."

"I set goals for myself," commented another, "-some short term, some long range. Progress has been steady ever since. The rally was six months after my loss. I would say-trust yourself. It will get better. Keep reassuring yourself that it will."

Isolation and withdrawal are problems for the lonely. This person knew that. "I dealt with loneliness by keeping busy in the church such as choir, circle, and morning musical club. I also sang in their chorus. I renewed my piano and voice practicing."

"The best way I found to overcome loneliness is helping other people."

"Plan ahead for things to do, however minor. Get involved in a redecorating project."

"One's relationship with friends and relatives is very important."

Another question I put to my friends was how long the intense pain lasted and what helped to lessen that pain.

Their answers ranged from two weeks to one year.

Listen to this idea that helped one person lessen the pain. "Physical exercise helped a lot. I sat in the sun and could feel the hurt being pulled heavenward."

I like this comment. "I learned to cry. I had never cried before. I went to church and cried. I talked to my friends and cried. I cried over old letter, pictures, TV programs and songs. I cried when I took his clothes out of the closet and bagged them. Getting my feelings out and putting them down on paper seemed to help to heal. The pain is still with me, but not so acute. The attacks don't come so often and they're beginning to take on a golden hue of lovely memories."

One woman who lost a child said that her acute pain lasted nine months - the same length of time she carried the child during pregnancy. She lessened her pain by reaching out to young people who had no place to go. She said, "All I am doing is giving away some of the love and comfort God has showered upon me."

Some people felt that getting back to work as soon as possible helped to ease the pain, but still others cautioned against going back before first working through the painful feelings.

A divorced person pointed out that changing patterns can alleviate pain and open new avenues of growth. "Because birthdays, anniversaries and holidays were such a happy, big celebration time for me, I deliberately try to push myself into doing things that don't in any way follow any "before" celebration lines. After two years, this year I found I got through our big birthday and anniversary month without being devastated. I realized that I can find enjoyment in doing things that are totally new to me."

One common denominator among most of my friends who shared with me is a fantastic philosophy of life and an attitude that has turned tragedy into a deep and meaningful life.

"I feel the Lord has a plan for my life and so I can relax about the future and live one day at a time. Also, I'm more aware of myself as a person and no longer just one-half of a couple. I've become more of an individual and a person with more depth. In truth, I like the person the Lord has allowed me to become."

The same person that shared the preceding words indicated that sharing them without getting depressed and uptight was an indicator of much progress.

One person's philosophy read, "Look on each day as an adventure, find something to enjoy, someone to love and a bit of good hard work to do- for someday tomorrow won't come and the world will go on without you."

As I read the letters from those who attended the Grief Recovery seminars, I realized that something had happened to me personally as a result of my friendship with them. I have become a wealthy man- wealthy in terms of understanding more deeply who I am. Wealthy in terms of having a broader circle of supporting relationships.

Take it from me - there is healing for those who grieve, and the healing results in a marvelous spirit of lifting another when he or she is down.

18

Sarah - Walls - Aggressiveness

Sarah lived alone in a weather-beaten house along the Ohio River. From the outside it appeared to be deserted. Weeds grew tall in the front yard. Window shades were faded and a few broken panes had been replaced by an old dress wadded up to keep out the rain.

Whenever I drove my car into her driveway, Sarah quickly came through the gate and met me under the old sickle pear tree. I was never invited into the house.

As I looked at her deeply wrinkled face and her deep-set eyes, I felt an icy wall separating us. She seemed afraid to trust me with anything except the usual prattle about the weather and the garden.

One evening my chance came to learn what made Sarah tick. I pulled into her drive ever so quietly. The raggedy old woman was bent over in her garden. When she saw me coming she picked up her bucket of potatoes and headed for the gate, but I beat her. I proceeded to the back door of the house.

"Oh, let me get that door for you, Sarah," I said quickly. "You've got a real load there."

As she went through the door, I quickly slipped through the door behind her. She dropped her bucket and turned to go back outdoors, but I was already inside her living room.

Embarrassment flushed across her face as she apologized for the disarray.

"Don't worry about that," I assured her. "I came to see you, Sarah, not to see how tidy your house is."

It was late in the year and there was no fire to take the chill out of the air. Sarah and I sat on straight-backed chairs and shuddered as we talked.

"Sarah, I don't know you very well. You seem to be all alone. Do you have any family nearby?" I asked.

"Nobody anymore. I had my husband, but he's been dead nigh unto 10 years now," she said in a forlorn tone of voice.

"It must have been very lonely for you all those years," I suggested. "Has there been anyone to share your heartache?"

Then came the story. The church folk didn't go to her husband's funeral. The preacher had the "service", but never came to see "how things were a'goin'." Anger about losing her husband was intensified by the neglect of friends. To avoid additional hurt, she quickly built a wall around herself. Ten years had made the wall almost impregnable.

I knew that Sarah would never reach out to others. She was a prisoner inside of her own walls.

"Sarah," I said in school teacher style, "I want you to listen real carefully to what I'm about to say. I'll let you know right off the bat that I'll not take 'no' for an answer. What you need is a good hot meal that you haven't had to fix yourself and a chance to spend a day relaxing and playing with children at your own pace. Now, you be ready by 10 a.m. on Sunday morning. I'm picking you up and you're going to spend the day at our house."

With that, I arose to leave, but Sarah went to her kitchen and sorted through the many bottles on her table. She dumped several large tablets into my hand. With a twinkle in her eye she said, "My word son, I should be ashamed to let you freeze like this. I'm afraid you've been chilled. Here, these rose hips tablets will ward off the cold. You can eat them on your way home."

She gave the response I was looking for. I knew that my persistence had paid off. The walls were not impregnable after all.

Oh, yes, I must add that the day was a huge success. My little boys were like good medicine to the old woman's broken spirit. The only thing she disliked was the icing on the chocolate cake. Too much sugar brought on the cold, she said.

Sarah's experience provides a lesson for those who grieve. It is so easy to isolate yourself from the world around you when your own personal world has been shattered. Wanting to withdraw to avoid further hurt is common. Becoming overly sensitive to the insensitivities of others often breeds self-pity, and self-pity is the material from which sturdy walls are built.

Let's go back to Sarah. I asked many of her acquaintances to fill in some background for me. I discovered that Sarah's anger about her husband's death caused her to display disagreeable traits that frightened them away. Their overtures were met with rebuffs, so they weren't about to return for another dose of the same treatment. Sarah had caused the disintegration of her small support system.

There is a lesson here for caregivers and the friends of those in grief. If you wait for an invitation from the brokenhearted, you may never receive one.

Grieving people say, "I don't feel like intruding on anyone." "Other people have their own lives to live." They don't want to have me crying on their shoulders." "I just feel out of place."

Caregivers must go out of their way. They must insist on drawing grieving persons into social circles again.

Look at icy walls as symbols of appeals for help. Let them be a challenge to you. Be innovative and find ways of winning the trust of the heartbroken. Insist on climbing the walls because there is human treasure on the other side.

To me, one of the deepest sorrows is to see a husband and wife building walls between them when they suffer the loss of a child. Intimacy and comfort is what they need from each other, but the wall only leads to further estrangement.

There is growing evidence that many of the marriage problems seen in offices of marriage and family counselors are caused by unresolved grief. Any competent caregiver will do a careful history of losses at the outset of the counseling program.

Addressing financial or sexual problems of a marriage in which many losses have gone unresolved is simply treating symptoms instead of the cause of disharmony.

In the usual course of marriage a person can look to his or her spouse for support and encouragement in a crisis. When the death of a child occurs, both spouses hurt so badly that they are often unable to render the usual support. This can cause resentment and anger which in turn blocks good communication. I advise grief stricken parents to seek the assistance of a counselor or a trusted friend just as soon after the funeral as possible. This prevents the erection of needless and destructive barriers.

Clergypersons and other professionals should be alert to the implications of poor grieving. These caregivers should go to the survivors with help instead of waiting until their cries of desperation are heard.

Quite a few years ago my wife and I received a call from our new Spanish friends. Their baby was stillborn. A Spanish-speaking pastor and I met the father and the funeral director at the cemetery. There we interred the baby in a little white box. The disappointed mother was too sick to attend the graveside committal.

A week later my wife and I took communion to the grieving parents. It was not easy for us to go, but we knew it had to be done.

Communion was rather anticlimactic after our greetings. The father and I embraced. The mother pulled my wife down onto the pillow with her where they wept together. The sobs of the aching hearts were followed by the quiet words - "This is my body which was broken for you. This cup is the new promise in my blood."

Little did we realize how our unrequested visit prevented isolation and wall-building in the lives of two people who were so very far away from homeland and family.

Early in grief is the time when people desperately want to talk. Walls do not go up at once. They are the result of weeks of isolation and being deprived of the chance for expression.

If intentional care is given early, there is no need for Sarahs.

19

A Miracle

Every time I see a broken spirit healed, I am convinced that healing of soul is one of the greatest miracles in God's repertoire. I do not doubt for a moment that God can heal a person who is afflicted with cancer or paralysis. I have witnessed this for myself, but such healings are not the greatest reinforcements of my faith.

To see a life that is broken with grief be given once again to others in love and creativity, is to me, the greatest evidence that God is not dead.

This miracle began to unfold before me when I was a very young boy. Every Memorial Day I helped my parents fill a large laundry tub with huge red and white peonies. Daddy loaded them into the trunk of the family car and drove us to the edge of our farm. There we quietly entered a tree-shaded cemetery where five small graves were marked with simple metal markers - "Yeagley."

As mother filled the vases with peonies she would retell the sad story of how five of the thirteen had died in infancy. The saddest of all was the part where two died close together and the bodies were on the front porch in cold winter. The preacher stood outside to conduct the funeral because of a scarlet fever quarantine.

When the fourteenth child was born, the doctor told us that little Audrey might not survive due to injuries suffered before her birth. Just weeks after the birth I saw my mother cradle little Audrey for the last time. She slipped into the peaceful sleep of death as Mother held her close to her breast.

At the funeral I sat close to the casket and cried while the organ played "lullaby and goodnight..." I looked at my parents and saw pain in the form of tears running down their faces. Six of the fourteen. How could there be any healing left?

My parents recovered and used the life that was still theirs to bless others. Scars - yes, but the hurt was gone.

Broken hearts are for healing. God is in the business of healing broken hearts. I saw this happen in the life of Maria who attended a Grief Recovery seminar. She introduced herself to the group.

"I am Maria," she announced, "and I had cancer of the breast a few years ago. I couldn't believe it at the time, but I felt sure they'd take care of it."

"Is that the most recent loss that you have experienced, Maria?" I asked.

"No. You see, I just came from the hospital a week ago and they told me I have cancer of the lung."

As she broke this news to us she was smiling and laughing in a nervous manner.

"I told the doctor I don't want those treatments," she continued. "I'll go through it without them."

Sitting next to Maria was a 14-year-old boy. It was his turn to introduce himself.

"I'm Joey. Ah-I-ah, I'm not as old as a lot of you here, but I've been having some trouble with sleeping and eating and all," he shared in a thin voice.

"How long has this been going on, Joey?" I asked.

"Well, it's off and on. Just about the time I think I'm OK, all of a sudden this comes on me. You see, my brother ran away from home four years ago and he hasn't come back. I never hear from him. My little sister-she died of leukemia three years ago. She was real sick." Joey paused at this point and put his head down. With a great effort he lifted his head and continued.

"I don't want to upset you or anything, but you see, my father murdered my mother two-and-a-half years ago. My sister and I came home from school and found her. We called the cops and they came and then my father got put in jail."

A great sigh came from his thin chest as he said, "Whew, I guess I never told anybody like this before. It feels good to get it out."

I looked over at Maria and noticed that she wanted to talk again. She told us more about her illness-again, with smiles and nervous laughter.

"Maria," I asked, "how is it that you tell us such a sad story with a smile and laughter?"

At that point the smile vanished from her face. A torrent of tears came. Angry words against doctors and family came pouring from her lips. The mask was taken away to reveal the ravages of the disease.

For the next four weeks Maria engaged in thinking, writing and talking. She participated in the group process. She was very honest about her feelings. I could tell that the slow process of healing was taking place.

Several months after the therapy sessions ended I received a phone call from Maria. She was hospitalized in another city. She asked me to visit her.

I entered Maria's room in the oncology ward. Her first words saddened me.

"Larry, the doctors just told me that the cancer has spread to my brain. I guess this is the last trip," she said. "But you remember how angry I was in our sessions. I want you to know that I am not angry any more. I was able to get it all out in those sessions.

Now I find myself having a lot of love for everyone. When the nurses are here I tell them that God loves them and I love them too. I told the doctor that the other day and he gave me a big hug and kiss before he left."

"Sounds like you've been doing a lot of growing, Maria," I added.

"Oh, I guess so. Larry, do you remember Joey?"

"How could I forget him?" I said.

"You didn't know it, but after our last session I hugged Joey with all my strength and told him that if I were twenty years younger and didn't have cancer, I'd be his Momma. I love that little boy."

As I left Maria I gave her a hug and kiss. She told me that God loves me and that she loved me too.

I walked to my car in a state of shock. I had just seen a miracle-the healing of a broken heart.

That night I received a phone call from Joey.

"Larry, this is Joey. You remember that Grief Recovery thing I went to? Well, I got a letter from one of the ladies saying she was putting $300 in the bank for me for when I go to college." His words all ran together.

"Did she sign her name?" I asked.

"No, Larry. There's no name, but I know who wrote it. It was that lady who sat next to me."

"Maria," I said to myself. "The miracle is now confirmed."

Helpful Exercise

1. Look back over your loss and your journey to adjustment. Make a list of the ways God helped you. You may want to write a prayer of gratitude. Celebrate your progress by planting a tree in memory of the person you lost. Use your imagination and celebrate in a manner that is suitable to you.

Epilogue

On the morning of October 14, 1980, our oldest son was killed instantly in a highway accident. He was 22 years of age. He had just completed B.A. degrees in theology and English and pastored a Seventh-day Adventist church in Corning, New York, for 15 months. Just a few weeks before his death he began working on the Master of Divinity degree at Andrews University in Berrien Springs, Michigan.

From the first day of life without Jeffrey, my family and I agreed that we would talk freely about his death and reminisce about his life. We agreed to respect each person's need to be alone and to allow the expression of feelings as well. Each of us had different space needs. It was very helpful to know that we had space when we needed it and closeness when we desired it.

I discovered that the strength of our marriage was the key to avoiding marital chaos. We found that all of the intimacies of our romance comforted us. We were not threatened by each other's grief. This ability to continue the closeness of romance has made it easier to be warm and supportive to the family.

From time to time displaced anger appeared. This caused some tension, but apologies were forthcoming. We rectified the troubled relationship as soon as possible. The longer we put it off -the more we collected extra baggage that robbed us of the support we needed. It also robbed our family of the love they needed so desperately.

Apart from the support my family and my friends gave me, I needed to commune with God in a very open and frank manner. I went to the park near my home where I was all alone. I audibly told God how utterly confused I was. I sobbed and begged him to give me peace. At one point I was so distraught that I leaned against a big oak tree. My chest was throbbing with pain and my head ached. Holding on to that mighty oak and claiming God's promise -"My peace I give unto you" -I thanked the Lord repeatedly for sending his healing into my life. I then shuffled over to a picnic bench and sat down. There I talked to God for a long time about my relationship with Jeffrey. I thanked God for the good times and asked him to forgive me for the times when I missed the mark as a father. From this time alone with God I gained strength to live through the funeral.

I did not fight back tears. If something happened to evoke

them, I let them flow. The urge to cry was my pressure gauge that told me to release the pressure.

Three weeks after the funeral my wife, Roberta, and I attended a Grief Recovery program that I directed. In the group were several couples who had lost a child. Some couples came the first evening specifically to be with us on the first anniversary of the death of their children. The support of other people outside of my immediate family has been indispensable in the healing process. The fact that we have a large circle of supporting and intimate relationships has been a lifesaver.

This has been the most painful experience of my life, but I am determined to allow the pain to happen. I have done nothing to avoid places, things and people who serve as reminders of Jeffrey. I talk about him to people who ask me about my welfare. I used his camera and I read his books. I read his journals and sermons. I listened to a tape of his last sermon and still listen to a tape of a song he composed. His school friends visited us frequently at our invitation. We shared memories of Jeffrey. I can assure you that experiencing the pain early and intensely in our grief brought about a mellowing of the pain.

My boys and I took a long walk in the forest the day after the funeral. We called it a walk in memory of Jeffrey, the hiker. We talked about how he was always out in front of the rest. His long legs were the first to reach the summit of a mountain. We walked with the same quick pace. At one point we climbed over a fence and ran through an open field and stood for a long time admiring a giant white oak. The wind at my face dried the tears as fast as they left my eyes. The tears were good. They were a celebration of life well lived. The grief was a celebration of love.

As we walked, we talked about how our dear Jeffrey was asleep in Jesus, quietly and peacefully resting until the resurrection. We shared our mutual belief that his first conscious act on resurrection day would be to look into the face of the Lifegiver. His voice, we felt, would be lifted in songs of praise to God. His big smile would be the same. His love of life would be the same. His adventuresome spirit would be just as high, and we'd take a brisk walk together through God's kingdom.

I have many unanswered questions on my mind, but I don't expect any answers until I can see the whole situation from God's perspective. In the meantime, I am experiencing the healing power of God in my life. That healing convinces me that God does not take life. It convinces me that God, in his omniscience, has a just and loving design in what he allows.

I discovered during this great loss how mature my sons are (I have no daughters). They showed tenderness and thoughtfulness almost beyond their years. If I had lost any hope in American youth, it would have been restored.

My experience has convinced me that educating people in the dynamics of grief can certainly facilitate the grieving when they suffer a loss. My involvement in death and grief education benefitted my entire family. Our understanding of our own feelings about death has paved the way for a smoother recovery.

The five of us in our family are all unique in our adjustment to Jeffrey's death, yet we are all adjusting.

The openness with which we have spoken about death and grief in our family was helpful to Jeffrey in his short career as a pastor. A month before he died, he conducted a week of spiritual emphasis in a private high school in New York. During that week he lived with the students.

One of the students was having a very difficult time adjusting to the death of a close family member. Jeffrey was a good listener. The student was able to get a lot of feelings out into the open where healing could occur. He pointed the young lady to some of the techniques in this book. Then he shared himself with her. He told her that he was not afraid to die because he had committed himself to follow God's will. He knew that, should death come to him, he would be given life that never ends at the resurrection.

That dedication of his life to God was renewed every day. The very last night of his life was spent discussing how God felt about his children. He went to his bedroom singing, "Jesus loves me, this I know, for the Bible tells me so." This simple children's song was his favorite carry-over from his childhood. His simple, strong faith enabled him to sing it without the slightest inhibition or doubt.

As I carefully reviewed the life of our son, it caused an aching void at times. Many times I raised my voice in praise to God for the gift of Jeffrey's beautiful life. More consistently each day I tell God to use me in any way he sees fit. I am determined that I will put as much into my life as possible so that God can say of my life what he will surely say of my son's life -"Well done, good and faithful servant. Enter into the joy of your Lord."

$7.50

❑ **Y**es, I would like ________ additional copy or copies @ ~~$6.50*~~ each postpaid (up to 10 copies) of **Grief Recovery**. Please send them as soon as possible.

Write for quotation on larger orders.

My check ❑ or my Money Order ❑ in the amount of $________ is enclosed.

SIGNED ______________________________ DATE ________________

ADDRESS ____

CITY ____

STATE ________________________ ZIP CODE ________________

ORDER FROM:
Larry Yeagley
520 N. Stine Rd.
Charlotte, MI 48813

. . . .

The author has written a manual that describes the grief support program he designed. The model is used in many hospices and churches throughout the United States and Canada. In the manual he talks about the dynamics of groups and the content of the 5-week support program. The program is flexible and easily adapted to a local situation.

❑ Please send me a copy of **Conducting Grief Support Programs**.

$15.00

My check ❑ or my Money Order ❑ in the amount of $~~12.00*~~ is enclosed.

SIGNED ______________________________ DATE ________________

ADDRESS ____

CITY ____

STATE ________________________ ZIP CODE ________________

*PRICES SUBJECT TO CHANGE.